Baec

MOSCOW

Imprint

Cover picture: St Basil's Cathedral, Red Square

100 colour photographs, 8 ground-plans, 3 special plans, 1 transport plan (Metro), 1 city plan

Conception and editorial work:
Redaktionsbüro Harenberg, Schwerte

English Language: Alec Court

Text:
Bernhard Pollmann

General direction:
Dr Peter Baumgarten, Baedeker Stuttgart

Cartography:
Georg Schiffner, Lahr
Falk-Verlag, GmbH, Hamburg (city plan)

English translation:
James Hogarth

Source of illustrations:
Historia-Photo (8), Jürgens (23), Pollmann (7), Sperber (62)

Following the tradition established by Karl Baedeker in 1844, sights of particular interest and hotels of particular quality are distinguished by either one or two asterisks.

To make it easier to locate the various sights listed in the "A to Z" section of the Guide, their coordinates on the large city plan (and on the smaller plan of the city centre) are shown in red at the head of each entry.

Only a selection of hotels, restaurants and shops can be given: no reflection is implied, therefore, on establishments not included.

In a time of rapid change it is difficult to ensure that all the information given is entirely accurate and up to date, and the possibility of error can never be completely eliminated. Although the publishers can accept no responsibility for inaccuracies and omissions, they are always grateful for corrections and suggestions for improvement.

US and Canadian edition
Prentice Hall Press

Licensed user:
Mairs Geographischer Verlag GmbH & Co.,
Ostfildern-Kemnat bei Stuttgart

Reproductions:
Gölz Repro-Service GmbH, Ludwigsburg

Printed in Great Britain by Jarrold and Sons Ltd, Norwich

0-13-058041-4 US & Canada
0 86145 414 6 UK
3-87504-109-7 Germany

Contents

Page
The Principal Sights at a Glance . . . . inside front cover
Preface 7
Facts and Figures 9
General 9
Population and Religion 11
Transport 15
Culture 16
Commerce and Industry 17
Notable Personalities 18
Rulers and Governments 24
History of Moscow 26
Quotations 35
Sights from A to Z 42
Practical Information 130
Useful Telephone Numbers 175
Plan of Metro 176
City plan . . . . at end of book

Preface

This Pocket Guide to Moscow is one of the new generation of Baedeker guides.

Baedeker pocket guides, illustrated throughout in colour, are designed to meet the needs of the modern traveller. They are quick and easy to consult, with the principal features of interest described in alphabetical order and practical details about location, opening times, etc., shown in the margin.

Each city guide is divided into three parts. The first part gives a general account of the city, its history, notable personalities and so on; in the second part the principal sights are described; and the third part contains a variety of practical information designed to help visitors to find their way about and make the most of their stay.

The Baedeker pocket guides are noted for their concentration on essentials and their convenience of use. They contain numerous specially drawn plans and coloured illustrations, and at the back of the book is a large plan of the city. Each entry in the main part of the guide gives the coordinates of the square on the plan in which the particular feature can be located. Users of this guide, therefore, will have no difficulty in finding what they want to see.

Facts and Figures

General

Capital of the USSR

Moscow (in Russian Moskva) is capital of the Union of Soviet Socialist Republics (USSR) and also of the Russian Soviet Federative Socialist Republic (RSFSR), one of the fifteen constituent republics of the Soviet Union. It is also the chief town of the Moscow region.
In 1712 Moscow was superseded as capital of the Russian Empire by St Petersburg. Two hundred years later, on 10/11 March 1918, the new Soviet government moved from Petrograd, as St Petersburg was then called, to Moscow, and on the following day, 12 March 1918, declared Moscow the *de facto* capital. Since 1923 it has officially been capital of the Soviet Union.

Language

The official language of the Soviet Union is Russian, but in each of the Union Republics the language of that Republic has equal status with Russian.
For the history of Russian language, the Russian alphabet, its transliteration and its pronunciation, see the section on Language under Practical Information.
Throughout this Guide, place names are given in their English translation or spelt out according to their approximate pronunciation.

Region

Moscow lies in the European part of the Soviet Union, which extends eastward into Asia. (In modern times the Urals have been regarded as the boundary between Europe and Asia; in antiquity the line between the two continents was drawn on the River Tanais: i.e. the lower course of the Don.) Geographically considered, Moscow lies in the Eastern European Lowlands. The geographical boundary between Western and Eastern Europe is usually taken as the River Vistula. From the political point of view the line between Western and Central Europe on the one hand and Eastern Europe on the other runs along the Elbe.
Within the Eastern European Lowlands Moscow lies between the Smolensk hills in the north and the Central Russian plain in the south.

Geographical situation

Moscow is situated in latitude 55° 44′ N (roughly the same as Copenhagen) and longitude 38° E, at an average altitude of 120 m (395 ft), on the River Moskva, a 502 km (312 mile) long tributary of the Oka which rises in the Smolensk-Moscow hills and is navigable downstream from Moscow.

Telephone dialling codes

From the United Kingdom: 010 7 (USSR) 095 (Moscow).
From the United States or Canada: 011 7 095.
For international calls from Moscow dial 07 (see Practical Information – Telephoning).

◀ *The Kremlin, seen from the River Moskva*

General

Area and population

Moscow has a population of 8 million within the 109 km (68 mile) long motorway ring which has marked its boundary since 1960, making it the most populated city in the Soviet Union as well as the one with the largest area. The pace of growth can be seen from the following table:

Year	Population
1812	250,000
1863	350,000
1882	750,000
1900	1,000,000
1917	2,000,000
1926	2,000,000
1939	4,100,000
1959	6,000,000
1971	7,500,000
1982	8,000,000

It is a striking fact that between 1959 and 1971 the population of Moscow increased by only 20 per cent, while over the same period all cities in the Soviet Union with populations of up to 250,000 increased by an average of 44 per cent, cities of a population up to one million by 38 per cent and cities of up to two million by 35 per cent. Still more striking is the small increase in population between 1971 and 1982. The explanation lies in an almost continuous ban on movement into Moscow. It is planned to keep the population and the area of the city constant until the year 2000.

Administration

Moscow is governed by the City Soviet of 1000 elected deputies and the District Soviets of the city's thirty-two districts or wards. The day-to-day administration is in the hands of Executive Committees elected from the membership of the City and District Soviets, which must report at least once a year to the Soviets; they must also report on their work to meetings of workers and to the general population of their areas.
All matters relating to the economy, culture, education, health, transport, building, the social services, trade, etc. are under the jurisdiction of the Soviets.

The different parts of the city

Moscow can be seen as a series of concentric rings with the Kremlin – an area of 28 hectares (69 acres) in the form of an irregular rectangle above the left bank of the River Moskva – as its focal point.

Central area:
The Kremlin is the geometric centre of a built-up zone some 4 km (2½ miles) wide which has grown up round it, and is bounded by the Sadovaya (Garden) ring of boulevards. Within this central area were the old settlements known by the names of Kitay-Gorod, Belgorod and Zemlyanoy Gorod.

Kitay-Gorod:
Kitay-Gorod, which extends north-east of the Kremlin, beginning at Red Square, is the oldest part of Moscow's central area. Originally a trading settlement, it is still the main business and commercial district, with banks, department stores and other shops, Government and other public offices, etc.
The boundaries of Kitay-Gorod follow the course of the defensive walls which were built between 1534 and 1538 in

order to bring the trading quarter within the Kremlin defensive system: on the north 25th October Street, which runs into Kirov Street, on the east the ring of boulevards, on the south the Moskvoretskaya Embankment along the banks of the Moskva. The name of Kitay-Gorod has no connection with China (Kitay in Russian): it probably means something like "middle fortress".
The walls were demolished in 1930. A short section has been preserved to the north of 25th October Street (adjoining the Metropol Hotel).

Belgorod:
Belgorod, the "White City", takes its name from the limestone walls built in 1586–93, following the Tatar raid of 1571; they encircled the whole of the built-up area north of the Moskva (the Kremlin, Kitay-Gorod, etc.). The walls, which had a total length of 9 km (5½ miles), were pulled down in 1775; their line is marked by the present ring of boulevards (Bulvarnoe Koltso). The name of the White City also bore reference to the fact that the inhabitants were "white" in the sense of being exempt from the payment of feudal-type dues. A settlement of this kind was known as a *sloboda* (liberty). The settlement of Belgorod was occupied by craftsmen, servants, etc., working for the Tsar, the high aristocracy and the Church.
In this area of present-day Moscow are the city's main shopping streets, the Bolshoy Theatre, the Lenin Library, the Puskin Museum of Fine Art, etc.

Zemlyanoy Gorod ("Earth Town"):
In 1591–92 an earthern rampart 14 km (9 miles) long topped by a palisade and defended by fifty seven towers was constructed round the area which came to be known as the *zemlyanoy gorod* or "earth town". The area south of the Moskva was now incorporated in the defensive system for the first time. This wall, which was pulled down in 1775 at the same time as the wall round Belgorod, corresponded to the Sadovaya (Garden) ring of boulevards which surrounds the whole of Moscow's central area. Among the principal sights in the southern part of the area are the Tretyakov Gallery, the Church of the Resurrection and the Church of All Afflicted.

Outer districts:
Between the Garden ring and the motorway ring which encircles the city is a zone some 13 km (8 miles) wide, now mainly built up, in which the fortified monasteries lay (many of them are still preserved) built to protect Moscow from Tatar and other attacks (Simonov, Novospassky, Andronikov, Novodevichy, Don, etc.). In this belt are to be found various satellite towns, villages, recreation centres and parks, the Television Tower, the Olympic Village, etc.

Population and Religion

Population

Of Moscow's 8 million inhabitants 3·9 million are employed, of whom 2·2 million are classed as workers.
Every year some 100,000 new dwellings are provided in Moscow, to be occupied by some 400,000 people. The city has at present 15·5 sq. m (167 sq. ft) of housing accommodation per inhabitant – the highest figure in the Soviet Union.

By the year 2000, the target date for the final achievement of the "Communist model city" (in President Brezhnev's words), every Moscow family is to have a dwelling of their own and every inhabitant is to have an average of 20 sq. m (215 sq. ft) of living accommodation and 30 sq. m (325 sq. ft) of open space.

Religion

The constitution of the Soviet Union guarantees its citizens freedom of conscience, "that is, the right to profess any religion or none, to practise a faith or propagate atheism" (Article 52). Religious propaganda and pastoral activity outside the church are, however, prohibited. The Russian Orthodox Church receives no financial assistance from the State but must depend on its own income from collections and other sources; it seems to do reasonably well on this basis.

To Lenin religion was a "cheap kind of vodka", to Marx it was the "opium of the people". Following the dictum "Philosophers have merely offered different interpretations of the world: what must be done is to change it", religion was considered in the immediate post-Revolutionary years as an anachronism which would soon disappear. Although religion has not in fact disappeared the estimated 20 to 40 million Christians in the Soviet Union are a minority social group. There are in total something like 1000 churches and 18 religious houses in which worship still takes place. Moscow itself has 47 functioning Russian Orthodox churches.

While under Stalin the Christians were persecuted and Khrushchov had 10,000 churches closed as "in need of repair", more recently the strategy has changed. "Anti-religious" propaganda is no longer permitted: what is allowed is "atheist" propaganda. "The incitement of enmity and hate in connection with religious beliefs is prohibited" (Article 52 of the Soviet constitution).

Russian Orthodox Church

Byzantium:
Unlike the Russian Catholic Church with Rome as its undisputed centre, the Eastern Orthodox Church never had a unifying central point. Different theologies grew up in different centres, all making claims to universality. We must think, therefore, of Eastern Churches in the plural rather than of a single Eastern Church. Thanks to its political power, however, Constantinople was able to establish its preponderant authority as the "Second Rome".

Introduction of Christianity in Russia:
Prince Vladimir I of Kiev was baptised in 988 as a preliminary to marrying the Byzantine Princess Anne. According to the Christian chroniclers the acceptance of Christianity was followed by a compulsory mass baptism in the Dnieper.

As the Church Slavonic language (see Practical Information – Language) introduced to Moravia in the 9th c. by Cyril and Methodius, the "Apostles of the Slavs", could be used in Kiev since it was understood by the Eastern Slavs, it was not necessary to make new translations of the sacred texts. The Christian missionaries (mostly Greeks and Bulgarians) were selective in the texts they made available to the Christians of Kiev, which in addition to the Scriptures themselves were confined to the legends of saints, sermons and treatises on Church law. Anything connected with the "Latins" was

People of Moscow

shunned, and the literature and philosophy of ancient Greece were also taboo.

Thus the new church in Kiev grew up in the image of Byzantine orthodoxy. The dogma, liturgy, law and constitution of the Byzantine Church were taken over, and the distinction between the ecclesiastical hierarchy and ascetic monasticism was maintained. The Kievan Church, however, was probably headed by a Greek missionary archbishop and totally independent of Constantinople.

Autocephaly:
This independence was established at an early date, but it was not until 1590 that the Oecumenical Patriarch of Constantinople recognised the Metropolitan of Moscow and All Russia as Patriarch of the Russian Orthodox Church, which thus became "autocephalic". Moscow now took over from Constantinople, which had fallen into the hands of the Ottomans in 1453, and became the "Third Rome".

Conflict:
The Church Slavonic translations of the Old and New Testaments and the Psalms showed divergences from the Greek originals. The conflicts to which this gave rise within the Russian Church – should a procession go in the direction of the sun or against it? should the sign of the cross be made with two fingers or three? – were settled at a Synod of 1653 in favour of Patriarch Nikon, who had been pressing for reform. Those priests who held to the old texts and liturgical forms became known as Starovery (Old Believers) or Raskolniki (Dissenters), and the resultant schism within Russian Orthodoxy has continued to this day. Perhaps the most popular defender of the old forms was Protopope (Archpriest) Avvakum (1621–82), who died at the stake for his faith.

Modern times:
In the reign of Peter the Great the Russian Church became a mere handmaiden of the State. From 1700 Peter left the Patriarchal throne vacant, replacing the Patriarch in 1721 by the "Most Holy Ruling Synod", an ecclesiastical college which was largely dependent on the Tsar. Later in the century Catherine the Great confiscated all Church property, and the Orthodox clergy became salaried employees of the State.
After the October Revolution the Synod was dissolved and the Patriarchal constitution of the Church re-established. In 1918 the Church was separated from the State: a separation now enshrined in the 1977 constitution: "In the Soviet Union the churches are separate from the State and the schools are separate from the church" (Article 52).

Church structure

The Russian Church took over from Byzantium the distinction between the secular clergy (the priests or "popes") who were strongly Russian in outlook, and the monks, who looked towards Greece. The priests, who must be married, do no pastoral work but confine themselves to celebrating Mass and dispensing the Sacraments. The monks, who are vowed to celibacy, fill the higher posts in the Church (the Patriarch, metropolitans, bishops, abbots, priors, etc.).

Liturgy

Since pastoral work plays no part in the Russian Orthodox Church, religious life centres on the liturgy, the celebration of the Eucharist and other services with prayers, singing and an elaborate ceremonial which is sometimes reminiscent of the pomp of a princely court. An important part is also played by the veneration of icons (see Practical Information – Icons).

The Church year

The central event in the Russian Orthodox year is Easter, to which the whole Church calendar is related. Certain festivals diverge from those of the "Latin" Church – the Descent into Hell (or Limbo), the Transfiguration and Mid-Lent, the mid-point of the Fast (the twelve-year-old Jesus in the Temple).

The Virgin plays a central part in many festivals, her status as the Mother of God being recognised as a dogma.

Transport

City transport

The main form of public transport within Moscow is the modern underground railway system (Metro), with almost 120 stations and a total network of some 200 km (125 miles). The city's buses, trolleybuses and (in peripheral districts only) trams are unlikely to be much used by Western visitors. Other forms of transport available are taxis and group or communal taxis.

Roads

Thirteen trunk roads from all parts of the Soviet Union run into the 109 km (68 mile) long motorway ring, which since 1960 has marked the municipal boundary of Moscow. The ring was completed in 1962.
The various ring and trunk roads are identified by white letters on a blue ground:
A=Boulevard ring
G=Garden ring
K=Motorway ring
M=trunk roads
The ring roads and the principal trunk roads have a special middle lane marked by lines. This lane is reserved for members of the government, diplomats, etc., and must not be used by other drivers.

Rail services

Eleven electrified lines from all parts of the Soviet Union run into Moscow's nine termini, all situated in the outer zone between the Garden Ring and the Motorway Ring (see Practical Information – Railway Stations).

Airports

Moscow is the focal point of all air traffic within the Soviet Union and an important centre of international traffic. It has four international airports.
Almost all Western visitors arrive at Sheremetyevo 1 International Airport, 30km (19 miles) north-west of the city centre (see Practical Information – Airports).
Other airports are Domodedovo (for the Urals, Far East, Central Asia and Siberia), Vnukovo 1, Sheremetyevo 2 and Bykovo (all for domestic flights) and Vnukovo 2 (State visits).

Shipping

Moscow has three large ports – the North Harbour on the Moskva Canal, and the West and South Harbours on the Moskva itself.
The 128 km (80 mile) long Moskva Canal, constructed between 1932 and 1937, links Moscow with the Upper Volga, making Moscow the Soviet Union's most important river-port. Since the canal thus provides a link with the Black Sea, the Caspian, the Baltic, the White Sea and the Arctic Ocean, Moscow is entitled to call itself the "port on five seas". Inland navigation is hindered, however, by long periods when the waterways are blocked by ice.
The canal was originally known as the Moskva–Volga Canal. It was given its present name of Moskva Canal (Moscow Canal) in 1947, on the 800th anniversary of the foundation of Moscow.

Sheremetyevo 2 Airport

In spring and summer motor-launches and hydrofoils ply on the Moskva, both as a regular form of public transport ("Moscow trams") and for the benefit of visitors (cruises, sightseeing trips).

Culture

Universities and academies

Moscow is the cultural and intellectual centre of the Soviet Union. Its seventy-five universities and other higher educational institutions have 645,000 matriculated students, including correspondence and evening students, and in addition there are some 240,000 scientific workers and scholars working in research and other institutes. This compares with the figures for the whole Soviet Union of 859 institutions of higher education, 4·6 million students and 1 million scientific workers and scholars. The largest universities are the Lomonosov University and the Patrice Lumumba University. Moscow is also the seat of the Soviet Academy of Sciences, the Academy of Art, the Academy of Medicine, the Agricultural Academy and the Academy of Educational Science.

Libraries

Moscow has more than 4000 libraries with some 300 million books. The largest is the Lenin library (see A to Z).

Academy of Sciences

Museums

There are about eighty museums in Moscow covering a very wide range of interests: history, the history of the Revolution, art, literature, the theatre, music, science and technology. The leading museums of art are the Tretyakov Gallery and the Pushkin Museum of Fine Art (see entries).

Theatres, music

Moscow has twenty-five theatres, including the internationally renowned Bolshoy Theatre (see entry).

Commerce and Industry

With 2·2 million workers (out of a total employed population of 3·9 million), Moscow is the Soviet Union's largest industrial city. It is part of the so-called "Industrial Centre", an area with a radius of some 1000 km (625 miles), the core of which is a zone round Moscow some 350 km (220 miles) in radius.

Roughly 12 per cent of the total industrial output of the Soviet Union is produced in Moscow. The most important branches of industry are metal-processing and engineering, car and truck manufacture, textiles, publishing and printing, foodstuffs and electrical engineering.

All Moscow's industry has been or is being moved out of the city itself.

Commerce and Industry

Economic system

The basis of the Soviet economic system is set out in the following articles of the 1977 constitution:

Article 10: The foundation of the economic system of the USSR is socialist ownership of the means of production in the form of State property (belonging to all the people) and collective farm and co-operative property.
Socialist ownership also embraces the property of trade unions and other public organisations which they require to carry out their purposes under their rules.
The State protects socialist property and provides conditions for its growth.
No one has the right to use socialist property for personal gain or other selfish ends.

Article 11: State property, i.e. the common property of the Soviet people, is the principal form of socialist property.
The land, its minerals, waters and forests are the exclusive property of the State. The State owns the basic means of production in industry, construction and agriculture; means of transport and communication; the banks; the property of State-run trade organisations and public utilities and other State-run undertakings; most urban housing; and other property necessary for State purposes.

Article 12: Earned income forms the basis of the personal property of Soviet citizens. The personal property of citizens of the USSR may include articles of everyday use, personal consumption and convenience, the implements and other objects of a smallholding, a house and earned savings. The personal property of citizens and the right to inherit are protected by the State . . .
Property owned or used by citizens shall not serve as a means of deriving unearned income or be employed to the detriment of the interests of society.

On collective farms see Practical Information – Markets.

Notable Personalities

Boris Godunov (*c.* 1550/51–1605) Tsar 1598–1605

Boris Godunov was a relative and favourite of Ivan the Terrible, though not belonging to the high aristocracy, and a member of the much-feared private army (dissolved 1572) of Ivan's personal domain, the Oprichnina. When Ivan was succeeded in 1584 by the feeble-minded Fyodor, his son by his first marriage with a Romanov, Boris Godunov became *de facto* ruler of the country. After eliminating all claimants to the throne and establishing his undisputed authority he had himself proclaimed Tsar after Fyodor's death in 1598 – the first Tsar not of the Rurikid dynasty. The kingdom he inherited was politically weak and economically ruined; and although Boris achieved great successes in external policy – both Russian and non-Russian observers praised his political and intellectual capacity – he had only partial success in restoring internal social peace.

His greatest domestic achievement was perhaps the creation of the independent Patriarchate of Moscow in 1589.
During his reign Boris was the target of numerous intrigues directed against him as a usurper, particularly by the Romanov family. The mysterious death in 1591 of Dmitry, Ivan the Terrible's youngest son, cleared the way for Boris's accession to the throne, and in 1601 he eliminated the Romanovs after a trial for witchcraft; but rumours continued to circulate that Dmitry had survived the attempt on his life, which inevitably was ascribed to Boris Godunov.
The supposed murder of Dmitry, the heir to the throne, and the appearance of a "False Dmitry" provided the theme for Pushkin's "Dramatic Chronicle of the Muscovite Kingdom, Tsar Boris and the False Demetrius" (1825). This tragedy and the "History of the Russian Empire" by N. M. Karamzin (1816–29) were followed by Mussorgsky's opera "Boris Godunov" (first performance in St Petersburg, 1874; now usually performed in Rimsky-Korsakov's arrangements of 1896 and 1908), which made the name of Boris Godunov internationally known.

Ivan I Kalita (1304–40)
Prince of Moscow 1325–28
Grand Prince of Vladimir and Moscow 1328–40

Ivan I fully merited his nickname of Kalita (Money-Bags). Skilful courting of the Khan of the Golden Horde earned him the commission to collect the tribute due to the Khan from the principality of Vladimir and the city of Novgorod. Of the money collected he was able to divert considerable sums into his own purse, enabling him to purchase extensive territories, from small villages and towns to whole principalities. Favourable opportunities for these acquisitions were provided by the splitting up of principalities as a result of the laws of succession. His purchases of land were consolidated by a shrewd marriage policy. He is accordingly known as the "first collector of Russian soil".
In 1325–26 Feognost (Theognostes), Metropolitan of Kiev and All Russia, chose Moscow as his seat as Ivan's policy of good relations with the Tatars seemed to him to make Moscow a safer place than the neighbouring city of Tver, and the Tatars had shown tolerance towards the Church. In the same year Ivan laid down the foundation-stone of the Cathedral of the Dormition, later to become the place of coronation of all Grand Princes and Tsars.
Thereafter Ivan acted as a kind of agent for the Khan (collecting tribute, etc.), and the *baskaks* who had been the permanent representatives or envoys of the Khan were gradually withdrawn. The Khan also presented Ivan with the "Cap of Monomakh" which remained the symbol of royal authority until Peter the Great's coronation as Tsar in 1724.
Ivan died in Moscow at the age of thirty-six and was buried in the Cathedral of the Archangel Michael in the Kremlin. He divided up his kingdom between his sons and his wife, and was succeeded as Grand Prince by his son Semyon.

Ivan III, the Great
(1440–1505)
Grand Prince of Moscow
1462–1505

Ivan the Great, son of Grand Prince Vasily II (1425–62), laid the foundation of the autocracy later practised by the Tsars, and made Moscow the strongest political force in Eastern Europe. During his reign almost all the Russian petty principalities were incorporated in the heriditary domains of Moscow. If Ivan Kalita is famed as the "first collector of Russian soil", Ivan III is the "collector of the Russian lands".

In 1472 Ivan took as his second wife Zoe (Sophia), niece of the last Byzantine Emperor. Sophia had been brought up as a Catholic during her exile in Rome, and her marriage with Ivan was engineered by the Roman Curia; but the Pope's hopes of gaining influence in Russia were disappointed when Sophia went over to the Russian Orthodox faith after her marriage. (Ivan's aim had been not only to "collect Russian lands" but also to free Christians in the conquered territories from the "scourge of the Latins", i.e. of the Roman Catholics.) It has been suggested that Ivan had seen this marriage as giving him a claim to the succession of the Byzantine Emperors; it is true that Byzantine Court ceremonial procedure was introduced at the Moscow Court and that the double-headed eagle became a royal emblem. But in fact Sophia had no claim to the Byzantine throne and played no decisive role at the Court, while the heraldic double-headed eagle did not originate at the Byzantine Court but probably stemmed from the Roman Empire.

One of Ivan's greatest achievements was to free Moscow from the overlordship of the Golden Horde. In 1480 he ceased payment of tribute to the Tatar Khan, thus shaking off the Mongol yoke; and seven years later he even succeeded in bringing the Khanate of Kazan under the authority of Moscow.

The expansion of the Muscovite kingdom made it necessary to reorganise the administration of the country. From 1500 onwards, therefore, Ivan installed administrative offices (*prikazy*) in towns and villages, with wide powers of control over the inhabitants and direct responsibility to him. He was assisted by a council (*duma*) of nobles (*boyars*) and high dignitaries, but this had little real influence on his decisions.

This strengthening of the royal authority, territorial expansion and consolidation of the princely State was accompanied, however, by a deterioration in the conditions of life for the peasants. In 1497 a new code of law (*sudebnik*) came into effect, in which, at Ivan's behest Russian customary law had been codified; thereafter free peasants were able to change masters on payment of the appropriate due only during the week before and the week after St George's Day (26 November). This made them almost totally dependent on the boyars and landowners and prepared the way for the later institution of serfdom.

In addition to his successes in external policy and these domestic policy measures Ivan is remembered also for the large-scale building activity of his reign which brought many architects, mainly Italian, to Moscow.

Ivan the Great died in Moscow at the age of sixty-five and was buried in the Cathedral of the Archangel Michael in the Kremlin. He had appointed as his successor – perhaps following Byzantine practice – not the relative next in seniority to him but the son of his second marriage who became Vasily III.

Ivan IV, the Terrible
(1530–84)
Grand Prince of Moscow
1533–47
Tsar of Russia 1547–84

Ivan IV, son of Grand Prince Vasily III (1505–33), was the first Russian ruler to be crowned as Tsar. His reign saw the development of the Russian "sacred absolutism". Apart from his domestic and external policies, his successes and, predominantly in his later years, failures, he is remembered mainly for the personality which made him one of the most unbalanced of Muscovite potentates and earned him the name of Ivan the Terrible.

Ivan's suspicious nature, persecution mania, violent temper and brutal cruelty are often explained as the result of a childhood during which he witnessed bloody conflicts between kinsmen, murders, arrests and bitter palace intrigues. He lost his father and became Grand Prince at the age of three, his father having followed the example of Ivan III in designating his eldest son rather than his next oldest relative to succeed him. His guardians were his grandfather Prince M. L. Glinsky and Prince D. F. Belsky. Ivan's mother Elena Glinskaya, as Regent, put an end to his uncle Yury's claims to the throne by having him arrested, whereupon his uncle Andrey took the oath of loyalty to his nephew.

When Prince Belsky fled to Lithuania in 1534, Ivan's grandfather attempted to seize power for himself but was arrested by Prince Shuisky and died in prison. The murder of Ivan's mother in 1538, when he seven years old, was followed by a palace struggle which went on for several years, mainly between the Belskys and the Shuiskys. After the arrest of Prince I. Belsky in 1542 the Shuiskys were for a time in the ascendant. In 1542 Ivan came under the influence of the new Metropolitan of Moscow, Makary (Macarius). A year later he had Prince A. M. Shuisky torn to pieces in the dog pound, and the Glinskys thereupon returned to power.

In 1547 Metropolitan Makary crowned the sixteen-year-old Ivan Tsar of All Russia, in a ceremony which showed Byzantine influence (as did the later style of "Tsar i Samoderzhets", corresponding to the Byzantine "Basileus and Autokrator"). During a great fire in Moscow in the same year the mob lynched Ivan's uncle Prince Y. V. Glinsky.

In 1549 Ivan deprived the boyars of their jurisdiction in matters of taxation, justice and military service over the "boyars' children" (the impoverished and dependent members of the boyar class) and thus considerably reduced their power. In the same year he appointed his own henchmen to key positions in government, a further blow to the authority of the boyars, and the Council of Boyars was now replaced by a "Select Council" presided over by Ivan's confessor Silvester. This displacement of the boyars was accompanied by the advancement of the "service nobility" (granted noble status as servants of the Crown) and the gradual establishment of serfdom on a legal basis. The new legal provisions were incorporated in the Sudebnik (Code of Law) in 1550.

The system of central government offices (*prikazy*) introduced in the reign of Ivan III was now further developed. The increased status of the service nobility was paralleled in the army by the special role of the regiments of Streltsy as the military élite. This consolidation of the absolutist autocracy within Russia made possible the successes of Ivan's expansionist policies in the conquest of the khanates of Kazan (1552) and Astrakhan (1556). But when the push towards the Baltic was crushed in the Livonian War (1558–82/83) Russia was politically and economically ruined.

In 1560 Ivan dismissed his confessor Silvester and departed from the moderate line of the "Select Council". Three years later, on the death of Makary, he was unable to find a Metropolitan prepared to support the Government. In 1569 he removed Metropolitan Filipp (Philip), who had openly condemned his despotism, from his post and had him murdered by a member of his private army, the Oprichniki; Philip was later canonised. In 1564 Prince Kurbsky fled to Lithuania and from there denounced Ivan's reign of terror. The Tsar then left Moscow, accusing the boyars of treason, but in 1565 returned

to the capital, having assumed full powers to liquidate the "traitors". Then followed a further reign of terror by the Oprichniki, involving the destruction of whole towns and the crushing of the boyars.
Ivan died in Moscow at the age of fifty-three. Some eighteen months earlier he had killed his eldest son Ivan, designated as his heir, in a fit of wild rage, and the throne, therefore, passed to his feeble-minded younger son Fyodor. The *de facto* ruler of the country was Boris Godunov, later to become Tsar.
Ivan was buried in the Cathedral of the Archangel Michael in the Kremlin. The Church of the Intercession of the Virgin, now St Basil's Cathedral, was built during his reign.

Vladimir Ilyich Lenin
(1870–1924)
Soviet politician

Lenin, founder of the world's first Soviet state, a giant figure who changed the face of international politics in the 20th c., was born on 22 April 1870 in Simbirsk (now Ulyanovsk), the son of a school inspector named Ulyanov.
A happy childhood in a strictly religious household and a successful school career came to an end in 1886 with the death of his father. Fifteen months later his elder brother Alexander was hanged in the St Petersburg fortress of Schlüsselburg as a member of a revolutionary group which had planned to assassinate Tsar Alexander III. The execution took place while Vladimir Ilyich was sitting his final school examinations. His sheltered life in a Lutheran family home was now at an end: as Lenin afterwards wrote, "My way in life was marked out for me by my brother".
The rest of the family moved to Kazan, where Vladimir Ilyich became a student at the University. As the brother of a convicted revolutionary he was kept under surveillance by the Tsarist secret police, and, after taking part in student demonstrations, was exiled to Kokushkino. In 1890 he was allowed to sit the State examinations at St Petersburg University as an external student, and in 1892 he took his degree.
In 1894 Lenin published his first work, "What are the 'Friends of the People'?", a critical analysis of the populist movement. In 1895, during visits to Germany, France and Switzerland, he established his first contacts with Russian exiles, and in the autumn of that year he founded the St Petersburg League of the Struggle for the Emancipation of the Working Class. Thereupon he was arrested and spent the years 1897–1900 in exile in Siberia, where he married Nadezhda Krupskaya on 22 July 1898. The works written during his period of exile were concerned not with a theoretical treatment of Marxism but with the attempt to evolve a practical scheme for agrarian Russia.
From 1900 to 1905 Lenin lived outside Russia. In 1902 he published (in Stuttgart) his "What is to be done?", in which he called for an organisation of professional revolutionaries. The Marxist party he had in mind must act as the vanguard of the working class; a socialist consciousness must be introduced into the masses from outside. At a congress held in London in 1903 the Social Democratic Workers' Party of Russia was split into the Bolsheviks (the men of the majority) who supported Lenin and the Mensheviks (the minority) who supported Martov. With the support of the Bolsheviks Lenin became *de facto* leader of the party.
After returning to Russia during the revolutionary uprising of 1905 Lenin spent a further period in exile from 1907 to 1917, during which the Bolsheviks consolidated their position as the leaders of a future revolution. After the outbreak of the February

Boris Godunov

Vladimir Ilyich Lenin

Ilya E. Repin

Revolution Lenin returned on 16 April 1917 to Petrograd (as St Petersburg was now called), where he was given a triumphal reception by the workers. In the same month he published his "April Theses", in which he saw the Russian Revolution as the prologue to world revolution. After the October Revolution he was elected head of the Government.
Lenin continued as leader of the party until his death, in spite of being crippled by two strokes (in 1922 and 1923). He died on 21 January 1924 of cerebral sclerosis, brought on, according to the official medical report, by "excessive intellectual activity". His embalmed body can be seen in the Lenin Mausoleum in Red Square (see entry).

Ilya Efimovich Repin
(1844–1930)
Russian painter

Ilya Efimovich Repin is the leading representative of the Russian Realist school. His genre scenes, historical pictures and portraits aroused not merely interest but enthusiasm and emotion both in Russia and abroad.
After studying at the Academy in St Petersburg Repin painted his best-known work, the "Volga Boatmen" (1872). His realistic approach caused a sensation in the art world of the day and was soon taken as the "programme" of the group who called themselves the Peredvizhniki (Itinerants). Although the official Press criticised his "profanation of painting" his importance was recognised and he was awarded a bursary for study abroad. After spending the years 1873–76 abroad, mainly in Paris, Repin returned to Russia and joined the artists' colony which the industrialist and art patron Savva I. Mamontov had established on his estate at Abramtsevo, near Zagorsk. From 1884 to 1907 he taught at the St Petersburg Academy (becoming a professor in 1893), and from 1895 to 1898 also directed the St Petersburg Art Studio run by Princess Maria K. Tenisheva, another generous patron of art.
Repin's sympathy with the poor and downtrodden ("Religious Procession", 1880–83) and with revolutionaries ("Arrest of a Political Agitator in a Village", 1878; "Unexpected Return of a Political Exile", 1884) can be felt in almost every picture he painted. The best example of the violent reactions which his unsparing realism could arouse is perhaps his picture of Ivan the Terrible with the son whom he had fatally injured (1885), which had to be protected by glass after a visitor slashed it with a knife (reproduction, p. 124).

Rulers and Governments

Principality of Kiev (Rurikid dynasty)	Oleg, the Wise	Prince of Novgorod	979–882
		Grand Prince of Kiev	882–912
	Igor (supposed son of Oleg)	Grand Prince of Kiev	912–45
	Olga (widow of Igor)	Grand Princess of Kiev (Regent for Svyatoslav)	945–62
	Svyatoslav Igorevich	Prince of Kiev	962–73
	Yaropolk Svyatoslavich	Grand Prince of Kiev	973–78
	Vladimir Svyatoslavich, the Saint	Prince of Kiev	978–88
		Grand Prince of Kiev	988–1015
	Yaroslav Vladimirovich, the Wise	Grand Prince of Kiev	1015–54
			. . .
	Vladimir II Monomakh	Grand Prince of Kiev	1113–25
			. . .
Vladimir (Moscow) and Moscow (Rurikid dynasty)	Alexander Nevsky	Prince of Novgorod	1236–51
		Grand Prince of Vladimir	1252–63
	Daniil Aleksandrovich	Prince of Moscow	1276–1303
	Yury Danilovich	Prince of Moscow	1303–17
		Grand Prince of Vladimir	1317–22
		Prince of Moscow	1322–25
	Ivan I Danilovich, Kalita (Money-Bags)	Prince of Moscow	1325–28
		Grand Prince of Vladimir	1328–40
	Semyon Ivanovich	Grand Prince of Vladimir	1340–53
	Ivan II Ivanovich	Grand Prince of Vladimir	1353–59
	Dmitry Ivanovich, Donskoy (of the Don)	Prince of Moscow	1359–62
		Grand Prince of Vladimir	1362–89
	Vasily I Dmitrievich	Prince of Moscow	1389–92
		Grand Prince of Vladimir	1392–1425
	Vasily II Vasilevich, the Dark	Prince of Moscow	1425–30
		Grand Prince of Moscow	1430–62
	Ivan III Vasilevich, the Great	Grand Prince of Moscow	1462–1505
	Vasily III Ivanovich	Grand Prince of Moscow	1505–33
	Ivan IV Vasilevich, the Terrible	Grand Prince of Moscow (Tsar from 1547)	1533–47
Tsars (Rurikid dynasty)	Ivan IV Vasilevich, the Terrible	Tsar	1547–84
	Fyodor I Ivanovich	Tsar	1584–98
(Time of Troubles)	Boris Godunov	Tsar	1598–13.4.1605
	Fyodor II Borisovich	Tsar	13.4–1.6. 1605
	False Dmitry I	Rival Tsar	20.6.1605–17.5.1606
	False Dmitry II	Rival Tsar	1606–10
	Vasily IV Shuisky	Tsar	19.5.1606–1610
(Romanov dynasty)	Mikhail Fyodorovich	Tsar	1613–45
	Aleksey Mikhailovich	Tsar	1645–76
	Fyodor III Alekseevich	Tsar	1676–82
	Ivan V Alekseevich	Tsar (nominal)	1682–89 (–1696)
	Sofya Aleeksevna	Regent	1682–89
	Pyotr I Alekseevich (Peter the Great)	Tsar (nominal)	1682–89
		Tsar (*de facto*)	7.8.1689
		Tsar (sole ruler)	1696 ff.
		Emperor of All Russia	2.11.1721–1725
	Ekaterina I (wife of Pyotr I)	Empress	1725–27

Pyotr II Alekseevich	Emperor	1727–30	
Anna Ivanovna (niece of Pyotr I)	Empress	1730–40	
Ivan VI Antonovich	Emperor (nominal)	1740–41	
Anna Leopoldovna	Regent for Ivan VI	1740–41	
Elizaveta Pyotrovna	Tsaritsa and Empress	1741–61	
Pyotr III (Duke of Holstein-Gottorf)	Emperor	5.1–27.7.1762	(Romanov-Holstein-Gottorf)
Ekaterina II (Princess of Anhalt-Zerbst)	Empress	28.7.1762–1796	
Pavel I	Emperor	1796–1801	
Aleksandr I Pavlovich	Tsar and Emperor	1801–25	
Nikolay I Pavlovich	Tsar and Emperor	1825–55	
Aleksandr II Nikolaevich	Tsar and Emperor	1855–81	
Aleksandr III Aleksandrovich	Tsar and Emperor	1881–94	
Nikolay II Aleksandrovich	Tsar and Emperor	1894–15.3.1917 (d. 16.7.1918)	

(Dates according to Gregorian calendar)

Sergey Yulevich Witte	30.10.1905–5.5.1906	Governments 1905–1917 (Prime Ministers)
Ivan Logginovich Goremykin	8.8.1906–23.7.1906	
Pyotr Arkadevich Stolypin	23.7.1906–18.9.1911	
Vladimir Nikolaevich Kokovtsov	23.9.1911–11.2.1914	
Ivan L. Goremykin (again)	11.2.1914–2.2.1916	
Boris Vladimirovich Stürmer	2.2.1916–23.11.1916	
Aleksandr Fyodorovich Trepov	23.11.1916–15.3.1917	
Nikolay Dmitrievich Golitsyn	9.1.1917–15.3.1917	
Georgy Evgenevich Lvov	15.3.1917–21.7.1917	Provisional governments
Aleksandr Fyodorovich Kerensky	21.7.1917–8.11.1917	
Vladimir Ilyich Lenin	8.11.1917–21.1.1924	Heads of government of USSR
Aleksey Ivanovich Rykov	2.2.1924–19.12.1930	
Vyacheslav Mikhailovich Molotov	19.12.1930–7.5.1941	
Iosif Vissarionovich Stalin	7.5.1941–5.3.1953	
Georgy Maksimilianovich Malenkov	6.3.1953–8.2.1955	
Nikolay Aleksandrovich Bulganin	8.2.1955–27.3.1958	
Nikita Sergeevich Khrushchov	27.3.1958–14.10.1964	
Aleksey Nikolaevich Kosygin	14.10.1964–22.10.1980	
Nikolay Aleksandrovich Tikhonov	23.10.1980–27.9.1985	
Nikolay Ivanovich Ryzhkov	27.9.1985–	
Vladimir Ilyich Lenin	Nov. 1917–2.4.1922	Communist Party chiefs, USSR
Iosif Vissarionovich Stalin	3.4.1922–5.3.1953	
Georgy Maksimilianovich Malenkov	5.3.1953–12.9.1953	
Nikita Sergeevich Khrushchov	13.9.1953–14.10.1964	
Leonid Ilyich Brezhnev	14.10.1964–10.11.1982	
Yury Vladimirovich Andropov	12.11.1982–9.2.1984	
Konstantin Ustinovich Chernenko	13.2.1984–10.3.1985	
Mikhail Sergeevich Gorbachov	11.3.1985–	
Yakov Mikhailovich Sverdlov	8.11.1917–16.3.1919	Heads of state of USSR
Mikhael Ivanovich Kalinin	30.3.1919–19.3.1946	
Nikolay Mikhailovich Shvernik	19.3.1946–6.3.1953	
Kliment Efremovich Voroshilov	6.3.1953–7.5.1960	
Leonid Ilyich Brezhnev	7.5.1960–15.7.1964	
Anastas Ivanovich Mikoyan	15.7.1964–9.12.1965	
Nikolay Viktorovich Podgorny	9.12.1965–16.6.1977	
Leonid Ilyich Brezhnev	16.6.1977–10.11.1982	
Yury Vladimirovich Andropov	16.6.1983–9.2.1984	
Konstantin Ustinovich Chernenko	11.4.1984–10.3.1985	
Anatoly Andreevich Gromyko	2.7.1985–	

History of Moscow

Dating

Dates are given according to the Julian Calendar until 14.2.1918, when the change to the Gregorian Calendar was made (see Practical Information – Calendar).

(1.9.5509 B.C.)

Creation of the world according to the chronology of the Byzantine era. All dates in the Russian chronicles, like the frequently quoted Chronicle of Nestor, are given according to the Byzantine era, which remained in use in Russia until the adoption of the Julian Calendar on 1.1.1700.

From *c.* A.D. 700

Varangians (Vikings):
The Varangians from Sweden are appealed to for help by the inhabitants of north-western Russia and enlisted as mercenaries in their internal conflicts. The term Varangian is derived from the Russian *varyag*, which itself comes from Old Norse *væring* (confederate).
The Varangians advance over the rivers Memel, Dvina, Velikaya, Volkhov and Dnieper and from Lake Ladoga into the interior of Russia, setting up fortified trading settlements and establishing their dominance over the local population. Their principal strongholds are Ladoga (on the lake of that name), Novgorod on the River Volkhov, Pskov on the Velikaya, Polotsk on the Dvina and Kiev on the Dnieper.

"Russians":
In the Frankish royal annals for the period 830–882, the Annales Bertiniani (named after the Monastery of St Bertin in Flanders where they were found), the "Rhos" are mentioned among those accompanying the Byzantine Emperor. It has been established that this mean Swedes, the term being applied by the Byzantines to the Swedes settling in eastern Europe. The Chronicle of Nestor also equates "Rhos" with Varangians.
The philologist W. Thomsen derives the Greek word "Rhos" from the Finnish *ruotsi* (rower, oarsmen). The Eastern Slav equivalent is "Rus", which has given us the term "Russian".
The names of the first Princes of Kiev are Scandinavian. Since the non-Scandinavian population paid tribute to their new masters the name "Rus" ("Russians") was at first confined to the Scandinavian ruling classes but was gradually extended to cover the whole population and the country.
The fact that the word 'Russians" originally meant Scandinavians and that the first Russian State was established by these Viking "oarsmen" gave rise to furious controversy among scholars, since the "Anti-Normanists" regarded the idea – broadly confirmed though it was – as defamatory of the Russian people.

852

This first date in the Chronicle of Nestor (a frequently inaccurate record) marks the beginning of the written history of "Rus".

c. 1080

The finding of a timber roadway dating from about 1080 within the area of the Kremlin suggests that there was a settlement on the site of Moscow in the second half of the 11th c.

In the reign of Vladimir II the principality is once again largely united under a single ruler. Vladimir's II's crown, the Crown of Monomakh, was worn by later Tsars of Russia. After Vladimir's death the political, cultural and economic decline of the principality of Kiev begins.	1113–25
First reference to Moscow in the Chronicle of Ipatyev, which records a feast given by Prince Yury Dolgoruky (Long Arm) in honour of the Prince of Novgorod. Yury Dolgoruky has since been regarded as the founder of Moscow, and the year 1147 has been taken as the date of its foundation.	1147
Prince Yury Dolgoruky surrounds the Kremlin hill with a defensive palisade.	*c.* 1156
The army of the Russian princes who have joined forces against the Mongols is routed in the Battle of Kalka. But when these mounted nomadic tribesmen – wrongly called Tatars – unexpectedly withdraw, the alliance of princes falls apart. Thereafter the history of Russia is fraught with rivalries and conflicts between the princes.	1223
Great Khan Ogodei, son of Genghis Khan, resolves in a council held at Karakorum to march against the west. The Mongol army is led by Batu Khan, grandson of Genghis Khan.	1235
Batu Khan takes Moscow. During the next hundred years Russland is exposed to widespread devastation and is completely isolated from Europe.	1237
Batu Khan takes Kiev. The Metropolitan flees.	1240
Batu defeats a knightly German-Polish army in the Battle of Liegnitz and the Hungarian army in the Battle of the River Sayo, but then unexpectedly withdraws, returning to Karakorum to take part in the election of a new Great Khan following the death of Ogodei.	1242
After returning from Karakorum, Batu establishes the capital of the Golden Horde at Saray on the Volga. The rulers of the various Russian principalities are required to appear before the Khan of the Golden Horde at Saray, where, subject to good behaviour, they are invested with the style and dignity of prince. The princes thus appointed by the Khan rule under the supervision of a *baskak*, an envoy or governor representing the Khan, who watches over their conduct of affairs and reports any deficiencies to the Khan.	1252
The Russian population is registered by the Khan's officials and is obliged to pay high taxes. The Church submits to the Mongol rulers, retains freedom of worship and is exempted from payment of tribute. Since no one can become Grand Prince unless he is acceptable to the Mongols there is bitter rivalry and much intrigue between the princes. The Khan plays one off against the other.	1257–59
Daniil Aleksandrovich, youngest son of Alexander Nevsky, Grand Prince of Vladimir, is granted the principality of Moscow.	1276

History of Moscow

1299	Maksim, the refugee Metropolitan of Kiev and All Russia, takes up residence in Vladimir, capital of the principality of that name, not far from Moscow.
From *c.* 1300	The only candidates for the dignity of Great Prince are the Princes of Tver and Moscow. The other Russian principalities are extensively devastated. Moscow, protected by its situation amid dense forests, receives a great influx of workers fleeing before the Mongols.
1317	Yury Danilovich, Prince of Moscow since 1303, marries the Khan's sister and is granted the dignity of Grand Prince.
1322	Yury Danilovich is compelled to yield up the title of Grand Prince to Tver.
1325	The Grand Prince of Tver murders Yury Danilovich, Prince of Moscow, and is executed by the Khan.
1325–40	Reign of Ivan I Kalita (Money-Bags)
1325/26	Metropolitan Pyotr transfers his residence to Moscow, thereby increasing the prestige of the Princes of Moscow. The foundation-stone of the Cathedral of the Dormition in the Kremlim is laid.
1327	Ivan I skilfully exploits a rising in Tver against the Mongol poll tax. The Mongol reprisals, in which Ivan himself takes part, entail the political and economic ruin of Tver, eliminating Moscow's only serious rival. Ivan's policies are directed towards good relations with the Mongols.
1328	Ivan Kalita becomes Grand Prince. The highest secular and religious authorities in Russia (the Grand Prince and the Metropolitan) are now both in Moscow. By securing large tribute payments Ivan gains the favour of the Mongols. He buys up towns and villages, becoming the "first collector of Russian soil".
1331	A great fire devastates much of Moscow, which is almost entirely built of wood.
1339	Rebuilding of Moscow and the Moscow Kremlim.
1354–78	Reign of Metropolitan Aleksky, who seeks to promote the national and ecclesiastical unification of Russia under the leadership of Moscow.
From 1357	Internal struggles among the Mongols strengthen the position of Moscow, which throws off the Khan's right to grant the style of Grand Prince.
1359	Grand Prince Ivan III is succeeded by his three-year-old son Dimtry. Metropolitan Aleksey takes over the government of the principality.
c. 1360	Aleksey founds the fortified Andronikov Monastery.
1362	On Aleksey's urging the six-year-old Prince Dmitry becomes Grand Prince of Vladimir.

Grand Prince Dmitry defeats the Mongols in the Battle of Kulikovo, on the Don – the first Russian prince to defeat a Mongol army. Moscow becomes the leader in the struggle to achieve national unity and the symbol of the fight against the infidal. Dmitry is now known as Dmitry Donskov (of the Don).	1380
To avenge their defeat at Kulikovo the Mongols lay siege to Moscow and burn it to the ground. Nevertheless Moscow remains the symbol of the national unification of Russia. The hereditary domains of Vladimir, and with them the dignity of Grand Prince, have now, *de facto*, passed into the hands of Moscow, which is the residence of the Grand Prince, although the title is officially attached to Vladimir.	1382
To protect the city against Mongol attack the wonder-working icon of the Mother of God of Vladimir is brought from Vladimir to Moscow.	1395
The conquest of Constantinople by the Ottomans means that the Russian Orthodox Church is now free of Byzantine control.	1453
The Synod of Russian bishops resolves that the appointment of the Metropolitan of Kiev and All Russia, residing in Moscow, no longer requires the approval of the Oecumenical Patriarch of Constantinople; the approval of the Grand Prince of Moscow is sufficient. The "autocephaly" of the Russian Church is thus established, but the Metropolitan is now dependent on the Grand Prince. At the same time the status of the Grand Prince is enhanced, putting him in the same position as the Greek Emperor in relation to the Patriarch. This development leads a hundred years later to the theocratic autocracy of the Tsars.	1459
The Metropolitan of Kiev and All Russia, residing in Moscow, assumes the new title of Metropolitan of Moscow and All Russia.	1461
Reign of Ivan III, the Great.	1460–1505
Ivan the Great marries Zoe (Sophia), niece of the last Byzantine Emperor.	1472
Ivan the Great summons Italian architects to Moscow; rebuilding of the Cathedral of the Dormition, building of the Kremlin walls, the Palace of Facets, etc.	From 1475
Ivan the Great ceases the payment of the tribute to the Golden Horde.	1480
Metropolitan Zosima declares Moscow to be the new Constantinople.	1492
Ivan the Great dies and is succeeded by Vasily III, his son by the Byzantine princess Sophia.	1505
The Pskov monk Filofey puts forward the theory of Moscow as the "third Rome" – "and a fourth there shall not be". This follows on Zosima's affirmation in 1492 that Moscow is the new Constantinople (which was the second Rome).	Early 16th c.
Reign of Ivan IV, the Terrible.	1533–84

History of Moscow

1547	Ivan is crowned as Tsar by Metropolitan Makary.
From 1550	The serfdom of Russian peasants is gradually given legal force. In parallel with the creation of a centralised adminstration and the granting of property to the "service nobility", the regiments of Streltsy (Marksmen) were built up as the élite of the army and the Tsar's personal bodyguard. Originally recruited from the urban and village population, they undertook a commitment to life-long service but enjoyed a fixed rate of pay and economic privileges. Service in the corps became hereditary.
1558–82/83	Livonian War. Ivan the Terrible at first achieves great successes, but under a treaty with Poland in 1582 and with Sweden in 1583 he is compelled to give up all his conquered territory. Moscow has now no access to the Baltic and is politically and economically ruined.
1560	Ivan the Terrible abolishes the "Select Council" presided over by his confessor Silvester and abandons the moderate line recommended by the Council.
1565	After his earlier "abdication" Ivan the Terrible returns to Moscow, armed with wide powers to liquidate "traitors". In order to ensure his possession of adequate resources Ivan takes over extensive areas around Moscow and in north-east Russia to form a personal domain, the Oprichnina. The boyars in these areas are expelled or killed, their property confiscated and distributed to Ivan's henchmen, the Oprichniki, who form a kind of private army.
1571	Tatars from the Crimea capture Moscow and burn it to the ground. Russia is again required to pay tribute.
1572	Ivan the Terrible executes leading Oprichniki and dissolves the organisation which he had himself created. The Tatars are defeated and compelled to withdraw.
1582	Ivan the Terrible fatally injures his son and designated successor.
1584	Ivan the Terrible dies, leaving his principality weakened both politically and economically, mainly as a result of the Livonian War. His feeble-minded son Fyodor is crowned as Tsar, but the real ruler of the country is Boris Godunov, who does not belong to the high nobility and is exposed to constant attack by the aristocracy.
1591	Dmitry, Ivan the Terrible's youngest son, dies in mysterious circumstances.
1598	With the death of Tsar Fyodor the male line of the Rurikid dynasty dies out. The "Time of Troubles" begins. Boris Godunov is elected Tsar by the Imperial Assembly, in which the service nobility is strongly represented. His election is thus probably due to his non-aristocratic origins and his good relations with the service nobility. He is the first non-Rurikid to occupy the throne.
1601–03	Famine throughout Russia leads to severe social unrest, particularly among peasants and Cossacks.

A Russian convert to Catholicism in Poland declares himself to be Dmitry, the son of Ivan the Terrible who was thought to have died in 1591. With Polish military help and a rapidly growing army of discontented peasants and Cossacks he advances on Moscow.	1604
Boris Godunov inflicts a crushing defeat on the False Dmitry's army but dies two months later. His son Fyodor is proclaimed as his successor but is quickly deposed. The Muscovite army, led by Vasily Shuisky, goes over to the False Dmitry, who is crowned in Moscow as the "rightful" Tsar.	1605
The False Dmitry marries a Polish girl, a Catholic. This triggers off a revolt by the boyars, and he is murdered. A second False Dmitry now comes forward, and like the first receives Polish military assistance. Vasily Shuisky becomes Tsar; but since he owes his election to the boyars, not to the Imperial Assembly, he is faced with rapidly growing opposition from the service nobility, peasants and Cossacks. The rebel army, led by a runaway serf named Ivan Bolotnikov, lays siege to Moscow. The rebels are defeated, but then rally under the banner of the second False Dmitry.	1606
Ivan Bolotnikov is taken prisoner, blinded and drowned. The second False Dmitry establishes a rival government at Tushino, just outside Moscow.	1608
The Romanov family enter into an agreement with King Sigismund III of Poland in the camp of the second False Dmitry: they are prepared to see the election of Sigismud's son Vladislav as Tsar.	1609
Tsar Vasily Shuisky is banished to a monastery and dies soon afterwards. Vladimir is elected Tsar. When the Poles occupy Moscow and Sigismund, with his own eye on the throne, seeks to prevent the coronation of his son there is a rising against the Catholic Poles, based on both national and religious feeling.	1610
The Russian armies take Moscow and the Kremlin; the Poles capitulate.	1612
The sixteen-year-old Mikhail Romanov, a boyar without princely status, is elected Tsar by the Imperial Assembly, founding the Romanov dynasty which is to rule Russia until 1762.	1613
Foundation of the suburban settlement of Nemetskaya Sloboda, on the River Yauza to the east of Moscow. The name is derived from the Russian word *nemets*, a dumb person, then applied to all foreigners who could not make themselves understood (it is now the normal word for "German"). On the insistence of the Church all foreigners are required to live in the new settlement. Nikon, a reformer, becomes Patriarch in succession to Filaret.	1652
Under Patriarch Nikon, following the reforming Synod of 1653, a schism develops in the Russian Orthodox Church. The liturgical texts are brought into conformity with the Greek originals.	From 1653

1666/67	Patriarch Nikon is relieved of his office by the Synod, but his reforms are made binding on the Russian Orthodox Church. The Old Believers reject the reforms and are thereupon excommunicated and persecuted.
1670/71	Stenka Razin leads a rising of peasants, Cossacks, Old Believers and the urban lower classes. He is taken prisoner and executed in Red Square.
1676	Tsar Aleksey dies and is succeeded by his eldest son Fyodor.
1682	Tsar Fyodor's early death leads to a struggle for the succession. The feeble-minded Ivan V and his brother Pyotr I (Peter the Great) are proclaimed joint Tsars, with their sister Sofya as Regent. The commander of the Streltsy leads a revolt and gains control over the government, but after a brief period of power is executed on the orders of the Regent. The "Table of Ranks", setting out the hierarchy of the nobility, service nobility, etc., is abolished and replaced by the principle of advancement according to merit.
1689–1725	Reign of Peter the Great.
1689	After banishing his sister Sofya to the Novodevichy Convent, Peter becomes *de facto* sole ruler (though his feeble-minded half-brother Fyodor continues to act as Tsar until his death in 1696).
1698	Peter has the rebellious Streltsy publicly executed in Red Square and dissolves the corps.
1.1.1700	Adoption of the Julian Calendar in place of the Byzantine era.
1700	After the death of Patriarch Adrian, Peter leaves the post vacant.
1712	Moscow is superseded as capital by St Petersburg (founded 1703).
1714	Peter prohibits the use of stone for building except in St Petersburg.
1721	The Patriarch is replaced by the Holy Ruling Synod, an ecclesiastical college controlled by the Procurator General, who in turn is responsible to the Tsar. Peter assumes the title of Emperor of All Russia.
1722	Introduction of a tax on beards.
1725	Death of Peter the Great, who had nominated no successor. His wife Catherine becomes Empress with the help of the Guards regiments commanded by Aleksandr D. Menshikov.
1727	Death of Catherine I. Menshikov is exiled. Peter the Great's grandson becomes Emperor as Peter II.
1737	A great fire destroys much of Moscow and the Kremlin.
1755	Foundation of Lomonosov University.

Reign of Peter III, also a grandson of Peter the Great. He is killed at the behest of his wife Catherine, a princess of Anhalt-Zerbst; but the belief persists among the people that he is still alive and will return to drive the "new Whore of Babylon" from the throne. — 5.1.–27.7.1762

Reign of Catherine II, the Great, the "foreign woman on the throne of the Tsars". — 1762–96

Church property is transferred to the ownership of a "College of Ecclesiastical Property" – amounting in effect to complete secularisation. — 1764

The Pugachov Rising: a rebellion by peasants, impoverished Cossacks and Old Believers led by Pugachov, a Don Cossack who claimed to be Peter III, Catherine's murdered husband. Pugachov publishes a manifesto against serfdom, which attracts further supporters to his cause. He is captured and publicly executed in Moscow. — 1773–75

Establishment of a censorship office in Moscow to check all publications. — 1796
Catherine the Great is succeeded by her son Paul I, a believer in absolutist autocracy.

Reign of Alexander I. — 1801–25

After Paul is murdered by a group of conspirators, including high officials and officers, Alexander becomes Emperor and introduces liberal reforms. The nobility recover their old rights, foreign books are permitted to be brought into Russia, a general amnesty is decleared, the use of torture in the trial of criminals is prohibited and the secret police is abolished. — 1801

Napoleon in Moscow. — 1812
Napoleon's Grand Army of some 160,000 men crosses the Niemen without any declaration of war, defeats Russian forces in the battles of Smolensk and the Borodino and occupies Moscow. Kutuzov, the Russian Commander-in-Chief, avoids decisive battles and uses the tactics of mobile warfare, taking advantage of the vast area of the country.
On 1 September Kutuzov evacuates Moscow, and during the next two weeks Napoleon enters the city with some 110,000 men. Difficulties of supply, the burning of Moscow, including the Kremlin, and the approach of winter lead to the withdrawal of the French forces, now numbering 100,000 in October. Under constant attack from the pursuing Russian armies the Grand Army is reduced to 37,000 men by the time it reaches Smolensk; after the crossing of the Berezina, it now numbers only 30,000 and completely disintegrates (November). Alexander is hailed as the "liberator of Europe".
The nobility and the officer class are influenced by the German idealist philosophers (Hegel, Schelling) and poets and writers (Pushkin, Gogol, Lermontov) by the European Romantic movement.

The growth of secret societies aimed at securing a constitution on the European pattern and the abolition of serfdom leads Alexander to abandon his liberal and reforming policies; he becomes the "gendarme of Europe". — From 1816

1825	Opening of the Bolshoy Theatre (January). Decembrist Rising: After Alexander's sudden death the secret societies take advantage of the turmoil over the succession to launch the Decembrist Rising in St Petersburg. Alexander's successor Nicholas I crushes the rising within a few hours; five of the conspirators (Pestel, Muravyov, etc.) are hanged and the others are exiled to Siberia. The Decembrists provide the model for all revolutionary movements aimed at liberation from Tsarism.
1826	Nicholas prohibits all discussion of the abolition of serfdom and re-establishes the secret police. Pushkin, Russia's greatest poet, sees the task as the "education of the people".
1849	The death sentences passed on the members of the Petrashevsky group (including Dostoevsky) are commuted to exile in Siberia.
1851	Opening of the railway between Moscow and St Petersburg.
1855	Death of Nicholas I. He is succeeded by Alexander II.
1861	Alexander's manifesto on the abolition of serfdom (leaving the ownership of land unchanged) leads to protests by peasants and students demonstrations, which are brutally repressed.
1862	Turgenev's novel "Fathers and Sons" is published in Moscow. The principal character becomes a symbol for the "Nihilists" fighting Tsarism and social injustice.
1866	Unsuccessful attempt on Alexander's life.
From 1877	Show trials of Nihilists, who are executed or sent to Siberia. Increasing numbers of secret societies are established (Land and Freedom, Northern League of Russian Workers, etc.).
1881	Alexander is assassinated in a bomb attack by the People's Will group and is succeeded by Alexander III. The terrorists are arrested and executed. Establishment of the Okhrana (political police).
1885	Student unrest in Moscow leads to the promulgation of "Rules for Students".
1917	October Revolution: fall of Tsarism.
1918	Moscow becomes capital of Soviet Russia.
1937	Opening of the Moskva–Volga Canal.
1941	Hitler attacks the Soviet Union (June). German troops advance to Moscow but are beaten back (December).
1951	The second Plan for the Development of Moscow is adopted (tower blocks in "wedding-cake" style).
1971	A new General Plan for the Development of Moscow comes into force.
1977	The Supreme Soviet of the USSR adopts a new constitution.
1980	The 22nd Summer Olympic Games are held in Moscow.

Leading politicians of the Warsaw Pact countries meet in Moscow on the seventy-fifth birthday of Leonid Brezhnev, head of State and party chief.	1981
Brezhnev dies and is succeeded by Yury Andropov.	1982
Andropov dies and is succeeded by Konstantin Chernenko.	1984
Chernenko dies and is succeeded by Mikhail Gorbachov as party chief and Anatoly Gromyko as head of State.	1985

Quotations

V. G. Belinsky (1811–48)
Russian literary critic

"As a result of the inevitable incursion into Moscow of Europeanism on the one hand, and the wholly surviving element of old-world conservatism on the other, it has emerged as rather an odd city, in which European and Asiatic features combine to dance in a gaudy haze before your eyes. It has spread and stretched over a vast area; what an enormous city, you might say . . .! Yet you have only to take a walk to discover that this sense of space is greatly favoured by the existence of long, exceedingly long, fences. There are no huge buildings; the more substantial houses are not exactly small, but then again they are not exactly large. They do not boast any particular architectural merit. Still striving faithfully towards the goal of domestic felicity, the genii of the ancient Muscovite kingdom quite clearly meddled in their architectural design. After an hour's walk through Moscow's crooked, slanted streets you will soon realise that this is a patriarchal, a family city; the houses stand apart, almost every one in possession of its own wide courtyard, surrounded by outbuildings and overgrown with grass."

Robert Byron
"First Russia, then Tibet"
(1933)

The Kremlin:
"Fantastic one has always known it to be from photographs. But the reality embodies fantasy on an unearthly scale – a mile and a half of weathered, rose-coloured brick in the form of a triangle that rises uphill from its base along the river. These airy walls, which in places attain a height of forty feet, are hedged with deep crenellations, cloven and coped in white stone after the Venetian fashion. Their impalpable tint and texture might suggest rather the protection of some fabled kitchen-garden than the exigencies of medieval assault.
But from their mellow escarpments bursts a succession of nineteen towers, arbitrarily placed, and exhibiting such an accumulation of architectural improbablility as might have resulted had the Brobdingnagians, during a game of chess, suddenly built a castle for Gulliver with the pieces. . . . Within the walls rose a white hill, as it were a long table covered with a cloth of snow, lifting up to the winter sky the residences of those vanished potentates, Tsar and God: to the west the two palaces, nineteenth-century Russo-Venetian, cream-coloured against the presage of snow in the sky; the little Italian palace of the fifteenth century, whose grey-stone façade of diamond rustications conceals the tiny apartments of the early Tsars; and then the Cathedrals: that of the Annunciation, with nine orange domes; that of the Dormition, where the coronations took place, with five helm-shaped domes; and that of the Archangel

Michael, whose central bulb stands high above its four smaller companions; nineteen domes in all, each finished with a cross, most of them thinly gilt; and then, higher than all, the massive belfry, crowned with a flat onion; yet still overtopped by the ultimate cupola of the tower of Ivan Veliki, colossal in solitude, the climax of this Caesearopapist fantasia. I looked down to the river below me; I looked up to the sky; I looked to the right and I looked to the left: horizontally and vertically, towers and domes, spires, cones, onions, crenellations, filled the whole view. It might have been the invention of Dante, arrived in a Russian heaven."

Lewis Carroll (1832–98)
English writer
Diary (August 1867)

"We gave five or six hours to a stroll through this wonderful city, a city of white houses and green roofs, of conical towers that rise out of one another like a foreshortened telescope; of bulging gilded domes, in which you see, as in a looking-glass, distorted pictures of the city; of churches which look, outside, like bunches of variegated cactus (some branches crowned with green prickly buds, others with blue, and others with red and white) and which, inside, are hung all round with *eikons* and lamps, and lined with illuminated pictures up to the very roof; and finally, of pavement that goes up and down like a ploughed field, and *drojky*-drivers who insist on being paid thirty per cent extra to-day, 'because it is the Empress's birthday'."

William Coxe
(1747–1828)
English historian
"Travels" (1792)

"A city so irregular, so uncommon, so extraordinary, and so contrasted, had never before claimed my astonishment. The streets are in general exceedingly long and broad: some of them are paved; others, particularly those in the suburbs, are formed with trunks of trees, or are boarded with planks like the floor of a room; wretched hovels are blended with large palaces; cottages of one storey stand next to the most superb and stately mansions. Many brick structures are covered with wooden tops; some of the wooden houses are painted; others have iron doors and roofs. Numerous churches presented themselves in every quarter, built in a peculiar style of architecture; some with domes of copper, others of tin, gilt, or painted green, and many roofed with wood. In a word, some parts of this vast city have the appearence of a sequestered desert, other quarters of a populous town; some of a contemptible village, others of a great capital."

Nikolay V. Gogol
(1809–52)
Russian writer
"Dead Souls"

A Russian meal:

"'Yes; pray come to table,' said Sobakevich to his guest; whereupon they consumed the customary glass of vodka (accompanied by sundry snacks of salted cucumber and other dainties) with which Russians, both in town and country, preface a meal . . .

"'My dear,' said Sobakevich, 'the cabbage soup is excellent.' With that he finished his portion, and helped himself to a generous measure of *nyanya* – the dish which follows *shchi* and consists of a sheep's stomach stuffed with black porridge, brains and other things. 'What *nyanya* this is!' he added to Chichikov. 'Never would you get such stuff in a town, where one is given the devil knows what.' . . .

"'Have some mutton, friend Chichikov,' said Sobakevich. 'It is shoulder of mutton, and very different stuff from the mutton which they cook in noble kitchens – mutton which has been kicking about the market-place four days or more. All that sort of cookery has been invented by French and German doctors, and I should like to hang them for having done so. They go and

Nikolay V. Gogol

Pyotr A. Kropotkin

Napoleon Bonaparte

prescribe diets and a hunger cure as though what suits their flaccid German systems will agree with a Russian stomach! Such devices are no good at all.' Sobakevich shook his head wrathfully. 'Fellows like those are for ever talking about civilisation. As if *that* sort of thing was civilisation! Phew!' (Perhaps the speaker's concluding exclamation would have been even stronger had he not been seated at table.) 'For myself, I will have none of it. When I eat pork at a meal, give me the *whole* pig; when mutton, the *whole* sheep; when goose, the *whole* of the bird. Two dishes are better than a thousand, provided that one can eat of them as much as one wants.'
"And he proceeded to put precept into practice by taking half the shoulder of mutton on to his plate, and then devouring it down to the last morsel of gristle and bone."

Aleksandr Ivanovich Herzen
(1812–70)
Russian publicist and revolutionary
"My Past and Thoughts"
(tr. Constance Garnett)

The French entry into Moscow, which took place in the year Herzen was born. He describes it in the words of his nurse): "At the beginning we got along somehow, for the first few days, that is; it was only that two or three soldiers would come in and ask by signs whether there was something to drink; we would take them a glass each, to be sure, and they would go away and touch their caps to us too. But then, you see, when fires began and kept getting worse and worse, there was such disorder, plundering and all sorts of horrors. At that time we were living in the lodge at the Princess Anna Borissovna's and the house caught fire; then Pavel Ivanovitch said, 'Come to me, my house is built of brick, it stands far back in the courtyard and the walls are thick.'
"So we went, masters and servants all together, thre was no difference made; we went out into the Tverskoy Boulevard and the trees were beginning to burn – we made our way at last to the Golohvastovs' house and it was simply blazing, flames from every window. Pavel Ivanovitch was dumbfounded, he could not believe his eyes. Behind the house there is a big garden, you know; we went into it thinking we should be safe there. We sat there on the seats grieving, when, all at once, a mob of drunken soldiers were upon us; one fell on Pavel Ivanovitch, trying to pull off his travelling coat; the old man would not give it up, the soldier pulled out his sword and struck him on the face with it so that he kept the scar to the end of his days; the others set upon us, one soldier tore you from your nurse, opened your

baby-clothes to see if there were any money-notes or diamonds hidden among them, saw there was nothing there, and so the scamp purposely tore your clothes and flung them down. As soon as they had gone away we were in trouble again. . . ."

Anthony Jenkinson
(d. 1611)
English merchant
"The First Voyage . . ."
(1557)

"The Citie of Mosco is great, the houses for the most part of wood, and some of stone, with windowes of Iron, which serve for Summer time. There are many faire Churches of stone, but more of wood, which are made hot in the Winter time. The Emperours lodging is a faire and large Castle, walled foure square of Bricke, high, and thicke, situated upon an Hill, two miles about, and the River on the South-west side of it, and it hath sixteene gates in the walls, and as many Bulwarkes. His Palace is separated from the rest of the Castle, by a long wall going North and South, to the River side. In his Palace are Churches, some of stone, and some of wood, with round Towres fairely gilded. In the Church doores, and within the Churches are Images of Gold: the chiefe Markets for all things are within the said Castle, and for sundry things, sundry Markets, and every Science by it selfe. And in the Winter there is a great Market within the Castle, upon the River being frozen, and there is sold Corne, earthen Pots, Tubs, sleds, &c. The Castle is in circuit two thousand and nine hundred paces."

Pyotr Alekseevich Kropotkin
(1842–1921)
Russian revolutionary
"Memoirs of a Revolutionist"

The district between Kalinin Avenue and Kropotkin Street:
"Life went on quietly and peacefully – at least for the outsider – in this Moscow Saint-Germain. In the morning nobody was seen in the streets. About midday the children made their appearance under the guidance of French tutors and German nurses, who took them out for a walk on the snow-covered boulevards. Later on in the day the ladies might be seen in their two-horse sledges, with a valet standing behind on a small plank fastened at the end of the runners, or ensconced in an old-fashioned carriage, immense and high, suspended on big curved springs and dragged by four horses, with a postillion in front and two valets standing behind. In the evening most of the houses were brightly illuminated, and, the blinds not being drawn down, the passer-by could admire the card-players or the waltzers in the saloons. 'Opinions' were not in vogue in those days, and we were yet far from the years when in each one of these houses a struggle began between 'fathers and sons' – a struggle that usually ended in a family tragedy or in a nocturnal visit of the state police. Fifty years ago nothing of the sort was thought of; all was quiet and smooth – at least on the surface."

Vladimir V. Mayakovsky
(1893–1930) Soviet poet

"The earth, as we all know, begins at the Kremlin. It is her central point."

Napoleon Bonaparte
(1769–1821)

A letter to the Empress Marie-Louise from Moscow, 6 September 1812: "I had no conception of this city. It possessed fifty palaces of equal beauty to the Palais d'Elysée Napoléon, furnished in the French style with incredible luxury, several imperial palaces, barracks, fine hospitals. All this has disappeared, for since yesterday fire has been devouring the city. Since all the little houses of the middle ranks are built of wood they catch fire like tinder. Furious at the defeat they have suffered, the Governor and the Russians have set fire to this beautiful city. Two hundred thousand citizens are in the streets, in despair and in wretchedness. For the army, however,

Aleksandr S. Pushkin

Lev N. Tolstoy

Lev D. Trotsky

sufficient is left; they are finding treasures of all kinds, for in this disorder everyone takes to plundering. The loss for Russia is immense; Russian trade will be ruined. These wretches have gone so far as to remove or destroy the fire brigade's pumps. I have got over my cold; my health is good. . . ."

"The Russians also greatly love tobacco, and formerly everyone carried some with him. The poor man gave his kopek as readily for tobacco as for bread. However, it was presently remarked that people got no good whatever from it, but, on the contrary, appreciable ill. Servants and slaves lost much time from their work; many houses went up in smoke because of carelessness with the flame and sparks; and before the ikons, which were supposed to be honoured during church services with reverence and pleasant-scented things, the worshippers emitted an evil odour. Therefore, in 1634, at the suggestion of the Patriarch, the Grand Prince banned the sale and use of tobacco along with the sale by private taverns of vodka and beer. Offenders are punished very severely – by slitting of the nostrils, and the knout. We saw marks of such punishment on both men and women. . . ."

Adam Olearius (1603–71)
"Travels to Muscovy and Persia"
(1656; tr. S. H. Baron)

"And now at last the goal is in sight: in the shimmer
Of the white walls gleaming near,
In the glory of the golden domes,
Moscow lies great and splendid before us!
Ah, how I trembled with joy
When this be-towered, shining city,
Bright-hued, imposing,
Once again, of a sudden, stood before my eyes!
How often, in profoundest grief,
In the night of my wandering fate,
O Moscow, have I thought of you!
Moscow: how violently the name
Plucks at any Russian heart!"

Aleksandr S. Pushkin
(1799–1837)
Russian poet

"It would be difficult to explain why, and where to, ants whose heap has been destroyed are hurrying: some from the heap, dragging bits of rubbish, eggs and corpses, others back to the heap; why they jostle, overtake one another, and fight; and it would be equally difficult to explain what caused the Russians,

Lev Nikolaevich Tolstoy
(1828–1910)
Russian writer
"War and Peace"
(tr. L. and A. Maude)

after the departure of the French, to throng to the place that had formerly been Moscow. But when we watch the ants round their ruined heap, the tenacity, energy, and the immense number of the delving insects prove that, despite the destruction of the heap, something indestructible, which though intangible is the real strength of the colony, still exists; and similarly though in Moscow in the month of October there was no government, and no churches, shrines, riches, or houses – it was still the Moscow it had been in August. All was destroyed, except something intangible yet powerful and indestructible.

"The motives of those who thronged from all sides to Moscow after it had been cleared of the enemy were most diverse and personal, and at first, for the most part, savage and brutal. One motive only they all had in common: a desire to get to the place that had been called Moscow, to apply their activities there.

"Within a week Moscow already had fifteen thousand inhabitants, in a fortnight twenty-five thousand, and so on. By the autumn of 1813 the number, every increasing and increasing, exceeded what it had been in 1812."

Lev Davidovich Trotsky
(1879–1940)
Russian revolutionary and Soviet politician
"My Life"

"The transfer of central government authority to Moscow was naturally a blow to Petrograd. There was great, almost universal, opposition to the move . . . The majority were mainly afraid that it would make a bad impression on the Petrograd workers. Enemies spread the rumour that we had agreed to cede Petrograd to Wilhelm. I believed, with Lenin, that the move to Moscow would not only ensure the safety of the government but also that of Petrograd. There would have been a great temptation to Germany, and also to the Entente, to gain possession, by a rapid stroke, of both the revolutionary capital and Petrograd. It would be a very different matter to take the starving city of Petrograd without a government. Finally the opposition was overcome, the majority of the Central Committee favoured the move, and on 12 March (1918) the government left for Moscow . . . With its medieval walls and its countless golden domes the Kremlin seemed a paradoxical place to establish a stronghold of the revolutionary dictatorship . . . Until March 1918 I had never been inside the Kremlin; and indeed I knew nothing of Moscow except one building – the Butyrki prison, in the tower of which I had spent six months during the cold winter of 98/99.

"As a visitor one can admire at leisure the historical monuments of the Kremlin, the bell-tower of Ivan the Great or the Palace of Facets. But we had to instal ourselves here for a long period. The close daily contact between two historic poles, between two irreconcilable cultures, was both astonishing and amusing. Driving past Nicholas's palace on the wooden paving, I would occasionally glance over at the Emperor Bell and the Emperor Cannon. All the barbarism of Moscow glared at me from the hole in the bell and the mouth of the cannon. Here Hamlet would have cried out, 'The time is out of joint; O cursed spite, that ever I was born to set it right!' But there was nothing of Hamlet about us . . . .

"The carillon in the Saviour's Tower was now altered. Instead of playing "God preserve the Tsar" the bells played the "Internationale", slowly and deliberately, at every quarter-hour."

The Alexander Garden, below the west side of the Kremlin ▶

Moscow from A to Z

*Alexander Garden (Aleksandrovsky Sad) H12(C1)

Location
Manezh Street
(Manezhnaya Ulitsa)

Metro
Biblioteka im. Lenina/
Kalininskaya

The Alexander Garden, an oasis of peace amid the turmoil of the city, lies below the north-west side of the Kremlin (see entry) walls, between Borovitsky Square and the Corner Arsenal Tower. The gardens were laid out in 1821 for Tsar Alexander I, after whom they are named, by Osip I. Bove (Beauvais), the architect responsible for the restoration of the Kremlin.
Before the gardens were laid out a little stream, the Neglinnaya, flowed by the Kremlin walls, forming a natural moat. It was bricked over in 1817–19 and now flows underground. A bridge built over the stream in 1516 can still be seen in the gardens, linking the Kutafya Tower in Manezh Street with the Trinity Tower of the Kremlin.

Tomb of the Unknown Soldier
(Memorial Mogila Neizvestnogo Soldata)

At the north entrance of the Alexander Garden is the memorial, in black and red granite, of the Unknown Soldier, commemorating all the nameless dead of the Great Fatherland War (1941–45). The memorial, unveiled in 1967, contains the remains of soldiers who died during the defence of Moscow in 1941. On the black granite slab burns the "eternal flame of glory". The inscription reads: "Your name is unknown, but your deed is eternal." The porphyry blocks, beside which the guard of honour stands, contain earth from the cities which were awarded the designation "hero city" after the Second World War.

Corner Arsenal Tower (Uglovaya Arsenalnaya Bashnya)

Above the Tomb of the Unknown Soldier rears the largest of the Kremlin's corner towers, the Corner Arsenal Tower, named after the Arsenal which lies immediately behind the walls (see Kremlin).
This 60 m (200 ft) high brick tower, with walls up to 4 m (13 ft) thick, was built by Pietro Antonio Solari in 1492. The original superstructure of 1680 was damaged in 1812 when the French tried to blow up the whole of the Kremlin, but was restored in its original form by Osip I. Bove.
A secret spring in the basement of the tower still survives. Its outflow into the Neglinnaya was walled up.

Middle Arsenal Tower (Srednaya Arsenalnaya Bashnya)

The Middle Arsenal Tower was built in 1495 under the direction of Alevisio the Younger (Aleviz Novy), who, after the death of his fellow countryman Pietro Antonio Solari, built the whole of the north-western section of the Kremlin walls with the exception of the Corner Arsenal Tower.

The tower was originally known as the Faceted Tower (Granovitaya Bashnya) after its striking faceted masonry.

Grotto

The artificial grotto at the foot of the Middle Arsenal Tower was constructed by Osip I. Bove in 1821.

Obelisk of the Great Revolutionaries and Thinkers

This triangular obelisk in the Alexander Garden was Moscow's first monument to the Great October Revolution. It was originally erected in 1913 to commemorate the 300th anniversary of the Romanov dynasty, but in 1918 the double-headed eagle which was the heraldic emblem of imperial Russia was removed and the obelisk was inscribed with the names of the great revolutionaries and thinkers of Socialism and Communism.

*Andronikov Monastery and Rublyov Museum M11/12

(Andronikov Monastyr, Muzey imeni Andreya Rublyova)

Location
10 Pryamikov Square
(Ploshchad Pryamikova 10)

Metro
Kurskaya, Ploshchad Ilyicha

Opening times
Thurs.–Tues. 11 a.m.– 6 p.m.

The Andronikov Monastery, above the River Yauza on the east side of the city, now houses the Andrey Rublyov Museum of Old Russian Art. The greatest of Russia's medieval icon-painters, Andrey Rublyov, was a monk in the monastery.

According to the old chronicles the monastery was founded about 1360 by Metropolitan Aleksey. It is believed to be named after its first abbot, Andronik.

Between 1410 and 1427, in the time of Abbot Alexander, the

A Moscow wedding ritual: a young couple at the Tomb of the Unknown Soldier

Cathedral of the Saviour, Andronikov Monastery

Icons in the Rublyov Museum of Old Russian Art

original timber-built monastery was replaced by new limestone buildings. It now served a defensive function, protecting the south-eastern approach to the capital. Andrey Rublyov, who spent his last years in the monastery and was probably buried here (d. 1430), almost certainly contributed to the decoration of the new buildings, the original painting of which is not, however, preserved.

Cathedral of the Saviour

The Andronikov Monastery, built more than half a century before the buildings of the Italian period in the Kremlin (see entry), offers an excellent opportunity of studying the pattern of early Moscow church-building. The best example is the Cathedral of the Saviour, built on a cruciform plan, with three apses and four pillars dividing the interior into nine compartments. The vaulting of the nave is higher than that of the aisles, and the corner compartments are lower still, so that, seen from the outside, the church rises in stages to its culminating point in the tall dome.

Other buildings

The most interesting building after the Cathedral of the Saviour is the brick-built Refectory, which dates from the reign of Ivan the Great (1504–06). Adjoining this on the east is the Church of the Archangel Michael and St Alexius (1694–1739), in the style known as Naryshkin Baroque. The tower was built by the Neo-classical architect Rodion R. Kazakov.
The monastery underwent much rebuilding and alteration in the course of its history but was restored to its original form in the 1950s.

Andrey Rublyov Museum of Old Russian Art

Andrey Rublyov himself, the greatest Russian icon-painter, is represented in the museum which bears his name only by copies (of excellent quality); most of the originals are in the Tretyakov Gallery (see entry), and there are other icons by Rublyov in the Cathedral of the Annunciation in the Kremlin (see entry). The large collection of original icons includes a "John the Baptist" which is attributed to Rublyov's school and a "Death of the Virgin" by Dionisy (end of 15th c.). Associated with the museum is a restoration workshop.

* Bolshoy Theatre

J13(D2)

Location
7 Sverdlov Square
(Ploshchad Sverdlova 7)

Metro
Ploshchad Sverdlova
Prospekt Marksa
Ploshchad Revolutsii

Although new productions at the Bolshoy (the Great Theatre or Grand Theatre) are infrequent, it is sold out every evening. The performances to be seen here are internationally renowned as the very acme of musical and dramatic perfection.
The Bolshoy, founded in 1776, moved two years later into its own theatre, which was subsequently burned down on more than one occasion. The present home of the world-famous opera and ballet companies is a Neo-classical building erected in 1856. It is fronted by a portico of eight columns with a low pediment bearing a bronze quadriga. The interior is lavishly decorated, with white, red and gold predominating. The auditorium seats more than 2000.
The Bolshoy ballet company usually performs in the Palace of Congresses in the Kremlin (see entry).

The Neo-classical façade of the Bolshoy Theatre

Performances by the Bolshoy Company are internationally renowned

Foreign visitors can get tickets for the Bolshoy through Intourist (see Practical Information – Information). In recent years the people of Moscow have increasingly tended to dress up for the theatre – though dinner-jacket and evening dress are not required.
Also in Sverdlov Square is the Maly (Little) Theatre (see Practical Information – Theatres and Concert Halls).

Central Lenin Museum (Tsentralny Muzey V. I. Lenina) J12/13(D1)

Location
2 Revolution Square
(Ploshchad Rovolutsii 2)

Metro
Ploshchad Revolutsii

Opening times
Tues.–Sun. 10 a.m.–7 p.m.

The Central Lenin Museum is housed in the old Duma (Parliament) building, erected in 1890. Since it was opened in 1936 it has had some 50 million visitors. Lenin's life and achievements are fully documented in the Museum's thirty-four rooms, which contain almost 13,000 exhibits – photocopies of his manuscripts, drafts of articles, notes, letters to relatives and associates, editions of his works in 118 languages, photographs, records, personal mementoes, models of the houses in which he lived, etc.
There is also a full-scale model of his study in the Kremlin (see entry), which can be seen only with special permission.
For Lenin's Funeral Train Museum (a branch of the Central Lenin Museum), see Practical Information – Museums.

*Don Monastery; Shchusev Museum of Architecture H8

(Donskoy Monastyr; Muzey Arkhitektury imeni Shchuseva)

Location
1 Don Square
(Donskaya Ploshchad 1)

Metro
Shabolovskaya

The fortress-like Don Monastery with its seven churches and twelve towers was the southern outpost in the defensive ring of six fortified monasteries designed mainly to protect Moscow from Tatar raids. Since 1934 it has housed a branch of the Shchusev Museum of Russian Architecture, which has from 1956 been associated with the Academy of Building and Architecture.
The monastery is at present in course of restoration – though the work is unfortunately not proceeding very rapidly. Almost all the buildings are open to the public, but in general effect the Don Monastery falls short of the restored Novodevichy Convent (see entry).

History

The monastery was founded by Boris Godunov, later to become Tsar, in 1591, during the reign of the feeble-minded Fyodor I Ivanovich. It stands on the site of the Russian army's position during the decisive battle with the Tatars in 1591, the last time the Tatar army advanced as far as Moscow. The monastery takes its name from a wonder-working icon of the Mother of God of the Don (Tretyakov Gallery – see entry) to which the Russians attributed their victory.
The Old Cathedral, built in 1591–93, remained until the end of the 17th c. the monastery's only building. The New Cathedral, in the centre of the square area enclosed by the defensive walls built between 1686 and 1711, was founded in 1684 by Sofya Alekseevna, Regent for her brother Peter I, and consecrated in 1698. Of the 18th c. buildings the most notable are the Gate-Church of the Virgin of Tikhvin and the West Gate, both in Naryshkin Baroque style.

Don Monastery: Gate-Church of the Virgin of Tikhvin and New Cathedral

Cemetery of the Don Monastery

New Cathedral

The New Cathedral (1684–98) is in the form of a Greek cross, with each arm of the cross terminating in a large apse and apsidioles flanking the apse on the east side. The Shchusev Museum is housed in the gallery surrounding the church.
The beautiful interior has a fine Baroque iconostasis with eight tiers of late 17th c. icons. Until the October Revolution the icon of the Don Virgin, now in the Tretyakov Gallery (see entry), was on the lowest tier. The frescoes on the pillars and walls, like the icons, date from the late 17th c.

Shchusev Museum of Architecture

The museum in the New Cathedral, a branch of the Shchusev Museum of Architecture (see entry), contains original drawings, plans, sketches, models and a large collection of photographic material on Russian architecture from the time of Peter the Great to the present day. There is also a model of a gigantic building which Catherine the Great planned to erect in place of the Kremlin – a plan which fortunately was never carried out. Also of interest are the plans by leading architects such as Shchusev, Osip I. Bove and Shchuko. A special section is devoted to plans, sketches and photographs of Moscow buildings which have been destroyed or demolished.

Sculpture

Scattered about the monastery precincts and in the cemetery are pieces of sculpture from monasteries, cathedrals, etc., which have been destroyed or demolished.

Cemetery

On the south side of the monastery is the park-like cemetery, notable particularly for its burial chapels and tombs of the Baroque period. A board at the entrance lists well-known people buried here (Osip I. Bove, relatives of Tolstoy, Turgenev, etc.).

English Inn (Angliiskoe Podvorye) K12

Location
4 Razin Street
(Ulitsa Razina 4)

Metro
Ploshchad Nogina

Just off Red Square, in the shadow of the gigantic Rossiya Hotel, is a white two-storeyed building with irregularly placed windows, approached by an external staircase. This is the old English Inn which was granted to the English merchants in Moscow by Ivan the Terrible in 1556. One floor was used as living quarters, the other as stores. It was here that English envoys would stay when on a mission to the Russian Court.
In the 17th c. the building was converted to other uses, and at the beginning of the 18th c. Peter the Great opened a School of Mathematics here. Subsequently the original building was lost to sight under later additions, and it is only recently, during the clearance of what had become a rather run-down area, that it was brought to light again and carefully restored. It now houses an exhibition of local archaeological finds.
Flanking the English Inn are the 17th c. Church of St Maximus and the 18th c. Church of St Barbara.

* Exhibition of Economic Achievements of the USSR J18

(Vystavka Dostizhenii Narodnogo Khozyaistva SSSR; VDNKh)

Location
Peace Avenue
(Prospekt Mira)

Almost every organised tour of Moscow includes a visit to the Exhibition of Economic Achievements. Here, within an area of some 220 hectares (545 acres), are displayed some 100,000

Metro
VDNKh

Opening times
Mon.–Fri. 10 a.m.–10 p.m., Sat. and Sun. 10 a.m.–11 p.m. Pavilions: daily 10 a.m.–7 p.m.

items, constantly being changed, which represent the latest achievements of Soviet industry, science and culture, transport and building. In addition to the 300 exhibition buildings and 80 pavilions there are a wide range of recreational facilities. The grounds are laid out like a park, with ponds and fountains, walks, cafés, restaurants and places of entertainment, as well as a large shopping centre and a fair.
Features of particular interest are the Sputnik Obelisk, a titanium-clad monument 96 m (315 ft) high (near the Metro station); the Museum of Space Travel; the panoramic cinema; and the monumental figures of the "Worker and Collective Farm Girl" (by Vera Mukhina, 1937), a characteristic example of the Socialist Realism of the Stalin era.
To see even a small part of this gigantic exhibition a full morning or afternoon should be set aside. A good way of getting a general impression is to take a trip on one of the electric trams which run half-hour sightseeing tours (fare 10 copecks).

Historical Museum

See Red Square

*Kalinin Avenue (Prospekt Kalinina)

H12–F12

Metro
Kalininskaya, Arbatskaya

Kalinin Avenue with its numerous shops is a good example of the juxtaposition of fine modern development and historic old Moscow buildings in the city.
This street, extending from the Lenin Library (see entry) to the Moskva, has an older and a new part. The older section, from the Lenin Library to the end of Arbat Street, still preserves the aspect of the past; at No. 5 is the Shchusev Museum of Architecture (see entry).

Kalinin Monument

In the gardens in front of No. 14 is a monument to the man after whom the street was given its present name in 1963: Mikhail Ivanovich Kalinin (1875–1946), who became an active Bolshevist in 1903, played a major part in the 1905 Revolution, and was Soviet Head of State from 1919 to 1946. Kalinin, to whom a special museum is devoted (see Practical Information – Museums), is buried under the Kremlin walls in Red Square (see entry).
No. 14 itself, a Neo-classical mansion which once belonged to a wealthy factory-owner named Morozov, is now the headquarters of the Union of Soviet Societies for Friendship and Cultural Relations with Foreign Countries.

House of Friendship with People's of Foreign Countries

The older section of Kalinin Avenue ends at an extraordinary building (No. 16), in the style of a Spanish castle with a riot of sculptural decoration, which also belonged to Morozov. It is now the House of Friendship with People's of Foreign Countries, in which a variety of meetings, lectures, discussions between artists or scientists, etc., are held. The building dates from 1890.

Arbat

To the left of the overpass which carries Kalinin Avenue over Suvorov Boulevard is Arbat Square, with the Arbatskaya Metro

Kalinin Avenue

station. Off this square runs one of Moscow's oldest streets, frequently mentioned in Russian literature, the Arbat, now known as the Old Arbat. Until the construction of Kalinin Avenue it was the city's principal shopping street and traffic artery.

From the Praga Restaurant at its near end the street follows an irregular course, with little streets opening off it on either side, lined with handsome old houses, many of them associated with notable people of the past (as can be seen from the commemorative plaques). The great poet Pushkin lived at No. 53 in 1831.

New Arbat

The name of New Arbat is often given to the ultra-modern section of Kalinin Avenue, the construction of which began in 1962. The team of architects who designed the New Arbat were awarded the Grand Prix of the Paris Centre of Architectural Research in 1966 for this magnificent example of modern town-planning.

Along the left-hand side of the avenue, which is over 80 m (260 ft) wide, are four huge buildings in the form of open books housing the offices of various Government departments. They are linked by a two-storey gallery 850 m (930 yd) long containing shops, restaurants, cafés, etc. Visitors who want to go on a shopping expedition will find almost all they want here – Russian souvenirs, delicatessen, gifts, books, cameras, etc.

At the near end of this section of Kalinin Avenue, on the right, is the little Church of St Simeon Stylites (17th c.), which now houses an exhibition by the All-Russian Society for the Protection of Nature. Carefully restored, this attractive limestone building fits surprisingly well into its new setting of huge tower blocks, each containing 280 flats.

At the west end of Kalinin Avenue, near the Moskva, rises a thirty-one-storey block (1963–70), the headquarters of Comecon (the Council for Mutual Economic Assistance).

** Kremlin (Kreml) H–J11–12(C/D1)

Metro
Biblioteka im. Lenina
Kalininskaya

Opening times
Daily 10 a.m.–7 p.m.

Admission free

A citadel looming over Moscow from its commanding position 40 m (130 ft) above the River Moskva, with the city's main streets radiating from it in all directions; a stronghold in the form of an irregular quadrilateral with an area of 28 hectares (70 acres); palaces and cathedrals, enclosed within a wall 2235 m (2445 yd) long, up to 19 m (62 ft) high and up to 6·5 m (21 ft) thick; a fortress ringed by twenty towers and gates: the Kremlin is the heart of Moscow, the soul of Russia, once the seat of the highest authority – over whom, in the words of a Russian proverb, there was only God – and still the centre of government.
The Kremlin is bounded on the south-east by the Moskva, on the north-east by Red Square (see entry), on the north-west by the Alexander Garden (see entry) and on the south-west by Borovitsky Square (Borovitskaya Ploshchad).

The term "Kremlin"

In 20th c. Western usage the term "Kremlin" has come to be used as a synonym for the government of the Soviet Union, but it was originally a general term applied to a fortified stronghold or district of a town (analogous to the acropolis of a Greek city), usually situated on high ground above a river or between two rivers (the Moscow Kremlin lay between the Moskva and the Neglinnaya, which now flows underground). The word "kremlin" may be derived from the Greek *kremnos*, a crag or steep escarpment.

The medieval Kremlin

The medieval Kremlin contained within its circuit of walls and towers the seats of secular and ecclesiastical authority and the residences of the country's rulers – a palace, government offices, a monastery, a church or cathedral, etc. This was the capital of the principality of Moscow as described in the first quarter of the 16th c. by an emissary of the Holy Roman Emperor, Sigmund von Herberstein: "On account of its size the castle may well be called a small town, for within its walls are not only the large and magnificent houses of the Princes but also the residences of the Metropolitan, the Grand Prince's brother and the principal members of the Council, who all have large wooden mansions here, and within the castle there are many churches."
When the Kremlin was rebuilt from 1475 onwards the highest secular and ecclesiastical authorities in the land, the Tsar and the Metropolitan, had their residences here; and the architecture of the Moscow Kremlin became the standard model for kremlins throughout Russia.
The huge area of the Kremlin reflected the requirements of defence at the time it was built. With the development of the cannon in the 14th c. the Kremlin had to be capable of withstanding artillery. The palace, churches and government offices had as far as possible to be outside cannon range, and accordingly an area of open space was left between the walls and the buildings within them.
It was only at the beginning of the 17th c., after the occupation

of the Kremlin by Polish forces and their subsequent surrender, that the old defensive structures began to give place to the palatial buildings which give the Kremlin its distinctive character today.

Early timber buildings

The earliest fortified structure is mentioned in 1156, in the reign of Yury Dolgoruky, who is regarded as the founder of Moscow. It lay near the present Borovitsky Tower and covered perhaps a tenth of the area now occupied by the Kremlin.
1238: Moscow is captured by Batu Khan and the Kremlin is burned down.
1239: the high ground between the Moskva and the Neglinnaya is surrounded by an oak palisade.
1325/26: the Metropolitan of Kiev and All Russia moves his residence from Vladimir to the Kremlin.
1326/27: Prince Ivan I Kalita erects the first stone building in the Kremlin, the Cathedral of the Dormition.
1331 and 1337: the Kremlin is devastated by fires.
1339: rebuilding (in timber) begins.

The "white" Kremlin

1367: Grand Prince Dmitry – later to be known as Dmitry of the Don after his victory over the Tatars – builds the first stone Kremlin. The white limestone of the walls led many travellers to call Moscow the "white city".
Subsequently various government buildings and churches are erected.
1397–1416: building of the Cathedral of the Annunciation.
1405: Feofan Grek (Theophanes the Greek), Andrey Rublyov and Prokhor the Elder of Gorodets decorate the interior of the Cathedral of the Annunciation with paintings.
1445: the Kremlin is almost completely destroyed by fire.

The "Italian" period

The years from 1474 to about 1530, during the reigns of Ivan III (the Great) and his son Vasily III, were a period of great building activity which largely gave the Kremlin its present appearance. Ivan the Great summoned architects to Moscow not only from other towns in Russia but also from northern Italy (the Milan school). The following buildings were designed by Italian architects:
1475–79: Cathedral of the Dormition (Aristotele Fioravanti)
1485–1516: walls (Pietro Antonio Solari, Alevisio the Younger)
1487–91: Palace of Facets (Marco Ruffo, Pietro Antonio Solari)
1505–08: Ivan the Great Bell-Tower (Marco Bono, known as Bon Fryazin)
1505–08: Cathedral of the Archangel (Alevisio the Younger)
The following were built by Russian architects from Pskov:
1484/85: Cathedral of the Deposition of the Robe
1484–89: Cathedral of the Annunciation
The buildings of this period, however, cannot be classified as belonging to the Italian Renaissance. To meet the requirements of the time and place the foreign architects had to find a synthesis between the Italian architecture with which they were familiar and the general style of the Kremlin as it had developed over the centuries.
In addition, the Kremlin now had not only to meet the requirements of defence, but also to reflect the power and dignity of the strongest State in Eastern Europe and the Russian Orthodox Church as the head of the "third Rome".

The Kremlin: general view from the Moskva

1500: the walls along the Red Square side of the Kremlin are completed.
1508–16: a moat 32 m (105 ft) wide and 12 m (40 ft) deep is dug below the walls on the Red Square side, linking the Moskva with the Neglinnaya.
At first sight the Kremlin and the town of Moscow seemed two quite separate entities: on the one hand the brick-built fortress looming over the town with its white cathedrals, on the other the low wooden houses of the ordinary people.
In fact, however, the town fitted into the general plan centred on the Kremlin: its streets radiated from this central point and surrounded it in successive rings (still recognisable in the Boulevard ring and the Garden ring).
The late 16th and early 17th c. were a period of decline:
1547: much of the Kremlin is destroyed in a fire.
1571: the Tatars of the Crimea take Moscow and devastate the town and the Kremlin.
1610: Polish troops occupy the Kremlin.
1612: Russian troops and partisans recover the Kremlin; the Polish occupying forces surrender.

Russian "fairy-tale" style

After the destruction wrought by the Tatars and the Poles the rebuilding of the Kremlin began, with more emphasis on decorative quality and less on the military aspects.
The feature characteristic of this period is the tall pyramidal tent roof, first seen in the Cathedral of the Ascension, Kolomenskoe

(1532), and found also on the central tower of St Basil's Cathedral (1555–60) in Red Square (see entry).
A further characteristic is the liking for decoration already mentioned. Stylistic elements, both external and internal, were taken over from palace architecture and used in building churches, with the object of creating a house of God which should surpass all secular buildings in splendour and magnificence. This "fairy-tale" style of church architecture prevailed until about 1680. In the 1650s it was banned by Patriarch Nikon; but in 1658 he was compelled to resign his throne. The fairy-tale style is the style generally thought of as typically Russian or Old Russian, which enjoyed a renaissance at the turn of the 19th c. A model was provided, once again, by St Basil's Cathedral in Red Square.

Buildings in this style:
1624–25: Saviour's Tower superstructure (Bazhen Ogurtsov, Christopher Halloway or Galloway).
1627: St Catherine's Church.
1635–36: Terem Palace (Bazhen Ogurtsov, Trefil Sharutin).
1635–36: Upper Cathedral of the Saviour.
1652: Pleasure Palace (Poteshny Dvorets).
In 1652 the reforming Churchman Nikon was elected and enthroned as Patriarch, and one of his first official acts was to ban tent roofs and all seductive and distracting ornament. He held that a monastery should preserve its monks from the

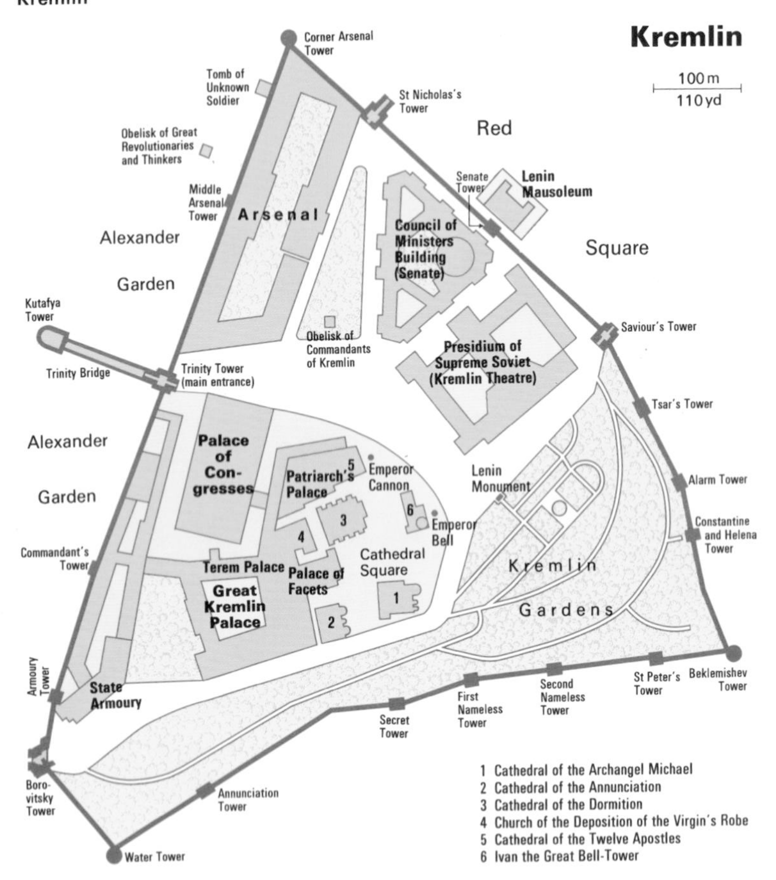

temptations of the world and not endanger their salvation by the lavish representation and display of fantastic and profane things. The churches of the "Italian period" were now to be taken as the model.

Typical of this period is the Patriarch's Palace, with the Cathedral of the Twelve Apostles (1653–56).

In 1658 Nikon resigned, and two years later was officially relieved of his post. Although in subsequent years tent roofs were little used, the decoration became still more lavish and more fantastic.

The towers on the Kremlin walls were given tent roofs between 1670 and 1685.

Naryshkin Baroque

After a time the stock of ideas of the decorative period were obviously exhausted and the first intimations of Europeanisation were unmistakable; and in the 1680s the Baroque style

came to Russia. The principal builder of secular buildings was a boyar named Naryshkin, a relative of Peter the Great, and accordingly the term "Naryshkin Baroque" is commonly applied to this period. Models were provided by architectural works imported from the West.
The surviving examples of this style in the Kremlin are mainly of the late 17th c., since after the transfer of the capital from Moscow to St Petersburg in 1712 Peter the Great forbade the building of houses in stone anywhere in Russia except St Petersburg (1714). Examples of Naryshkin Baroque in the Kremlin are:
1680–81: Church of the Resurrection (Terem Palace).
1681: Church of the Crucifixion (Terem Palace).
1702–36: Arsenal.

Neo-classicism

In 1762 Tsar Peter III issued a declaration abolishing the obligation on the nobility to enter the imperial service, and in the same year a number of ordinances were proclaimed abolishing the crown's trade monopolies. After her *coup d'état* in June 1762 Catherine the Great continued this policy of promoting Russian trade. As a result the nobility began to go in for trade, and architecture showed a movement away from the decorative and the Baroque and towards a more balanced and clearly articulated style of building.
1773: a general rebuilding of the Kremlin in Neo-classical style is planned in the reign of Catherine the Great. It is, fortunately, not carried out, but some of the towers on the Moskva side are destroyed during preparatory work.
1776–88: the Senate (now occupied by the Council of Ministers of the USSR) is built.
1812: Napoleon, before leaving the smoking ruins of Moscow with his Grand Army, orders the Kremlin to be blown up. The people of Moscow sabotage most of the operation, but the Water Tower, the First Nameless Tower and the Ivan the Great Bell-Tower are blown up.
1813–18: the Kremlin is restored and the moat on the Red Square side is filled in. The damaged towers are restored under the direction of Osip I. Bove.
1817–19: the Neglinnaya is covered over and now flows underground in a brick conduit.
1821: the Alexander Garden (see entry) is laid out by Osip I. Bove.
1825: the restoration of the Kremlin is for all practical purposes complete.

Later buildings:
1838–49: Great Kremlin Palace (Konstantin A. Thon, Nikolay I. Chichagov and others).
1844–51: State Armoury (Thon, Chichagov and others).

20th c.

The post-Revolutionary period has been mainly concerned with restoration and renovation work in the Kremlin. This work has restored the Kremlin, not perhaps to its old splendour but to a new splendour which it has not known for centuries. The churches have been restored and frescoes exposed, though the tasteless alterations of Nicholas I's reign cannot be reversed and a number of historic old buildings have been lost.
Two monasteries have been demolished, but the other cathedrals are now mostly museums, well cared for by their directors.

New work during this period:
1932–34: Presidium of the Supreme Soviet (originally designed as government offices), with the Kremlin Theatre.
1937: the towers are topped by five-pointed Soviet stars, which revolve slowly and are illuminated at night.
1960–61: Palace of Congresses.

Visiting arrangements

The following entrances to the Kremlin are open to the public from 10 a.m. to 7 p.m. without interruption:
Saviour's Tower (from Red Square – see entry)
Kutafya Tower (from Manezh Street and the Alexander Garden – see entry)
Borovitsky Tower (from Borovitsky Square)
The starting and finishing point of all conducted tours of the Kremlin is the Borovitsky Tower, on the west side. This is also the entrance for visitors who want to see only the Armoury.
Toilet facilities and a left luggage office (where large bags, etc., must be left) are in the Kutafya Tower.
Closed areas:
Some buildings, including the government buildings, can be seen only with special permission (apply to Intourist: see Practical Information – Information). The public are admitted to the Palace of Congresses and the Presidium of the Supreme Soviet (Kremlin Theatre) in the evenings for dramatic performances, concerts and film shows.
The closed areas are marked by white lines; there is usually also a sentry. It is forbidden to enter a closed area.
Photography:
Taking photographs is permitted except in closed areas. It is prohibited in almost all museums (including the cathedrals). Colour slides are on sale in kiosks outside the museums and cathedrals. See also Practical Information – Photography.

Borovitsky Tower (Borovitskaya Bashnya)

Location
Borovitsky Square
(Borovitskaya Ploshchad)

Metro
Biblioteka im. Lenina

Opening times
Sat.–Thurs. 10 a.m.–7 p.m.

The Borovitsky Gate-Tower, at the west end of the Kremlin walls, was erected in 1490 during the rebuilding of the Kremlin by Pietro Antonio Solari. It is a massive cubic structure built in brick with a series of receding storeys. The tent-roofed superstructure was added in the 1670s, when almost all the Kremlin towers received their present roofs. Like many of the towers, the Borovitsky Tower is topped by a five-pointed Soviet star, 3 m (10 ft) high and weighing 1·5 tonnes, which is illuminated at night. The total height of the Borovitsky Tower is 50·7 m (166 ft).

The tower occupies the position of the oldest entrance to the Kremlin. Its name is derived from the word *bor* (forest) – suggesting that the original settlement on the site of Moscow was established in this wooded area (now represented only by a few trees), on the Neglinnaya and near the Moskva, by people who lived by hunting and fishing.

The gate-tower

In addition to the normal gateway flanked by towers the Kremlin gates originally had the additional protection of a barbican or outwork. These (none of which survive) were usually in front of the gate; in the case of the Borovitsky Tower the barbican was on one side. The chains of the drawbridge over the Neglinnaya ran through openings in the front of the gate.

Entrances to the Kremlin: the Kutafya Tower (left) and the Borovitsky Tower

The passage through the barbican had portcullises, which could be lowered on the approach of an enemy. The space thus enclosed, with embrasures and machicolations, could be kept under surveillance from above.

The walls

The distance between the towers was determined by the range of the firearms then available. The towers also served as buttresses to increase the strength of the walls.
Along the top of the walls between the towers ran wall-walks with swallow-tail battlements up to 2·5 m (8 ft) high, embrasures and a wooden roof.

**State Armoury (Oruzheinaya Palata)

Opening times
Sat.–Thurs. (conducted tours only)

Conducted tours
Sat.–Thurs. at 9.30 and 11.30 a.m., 2.30 and 4.30 p.m. (English-speaking guides)

Admission charge
30 copecks

The State Armoury is the oldest museum in the Soviet Union and one of the richest. Among its treasures are the crown jewels and coronation insignia of the Tsars, historic arms and armour, costumes and furnishings, icons and manuscripts, coaches, sleighs, State carriages, *objet d'art* and much else besides.
The collection includes not only Russian art but the arts and crafts of Western and Northern Europe and the East as well. The Armoury's displays of English silver and German goldsmiths' work of the Baroque period, for example, are among the finest collections of the kind in the world.

History

Although the Armoury has for centuries been a museum it still preserves its old name. Here in the time of the Princes, Grand Princes and Tsars arms and armour were made and stored.

Main front of the Armoury

The royal insignia of Mikhail Romanov

The collection dates from the time of Ivan the Great and Ivan the Terrible. During the "Italian period" a special stone building was erected to house the Tsars' treasures. The original collection of arms and armour, military booty, royal insignia, gifts to the Tsar, carriages, etc., grew to such an extent that when it was moved to Novgorod in 1571 to escape the Tatars no fewer than 450 sleighs were required to transport it.
The heyday of the Armoury was in the second half of the 17th c. In 1654 Bogdan Khitrovo was appointed Director, and under his management the most talented craftsmen and painters in the old Russian art centres (Yaroslavl, Ustyug, Uglich, etc.) were summoned to Moscow to work in the Armoury.
When St Petersburg became the capital in 1712 the artists and craftsmen left Moscow for the new capital. In 1812, when Napoleon was advancing on Moscow, most of the Armoury's treasures were evacuated to Nizhny Novgorod (now Gorky) for safety, to be brought back in the following year.
The present Armoury building, in pseudo-Russian style, with features borrowed from Naryshkin Baroque, was erected between 1844 and 1851; the architects were Konstantin A. Thon, Nikolay I. Chichagov and Vladimir A. Bakarev. It is in architectural harmony with the Great Kremlin Palace, also designed by Thon and Chichagov.
Until the October Revolution the Armoury housed the Court Museum. After the Revolution the collections were enriched by treasures from the Kremlin cathedrals and the Patriarchal Treasury and by the crown jewels. Thereafter the museum was completely reorganised – a process which was completed in 1961.

Ground floor
Thrones of Russian Tsars and royal insignia:

Room 5

The ivory throne of Ivan the Terrible; Boris Godunov's throne (wood, covered with gold-leaf; more than 2000 precious stones); the throne of Mikhail Fyodorovich, the first Romanov Tsar; the Diamond Throne of Tsar Aleksey Mikhailovich (over 8000 diamonds); the triple throne of the joint Tsars Ivan V and Peter I and their sister and Regent Sofya Alekseevna.

Cap of Monomakh:
The Cap (or Crown) of Monomakh is believed to have been a gift from the Tatar Khan to Grand Prince Ivan I Kalita. It was used in the coronation of all Grand Princes of Moscow and Tsars of Russia until Peter the Great's coronation as Emperor in 1721. It is probably 14th c. Oriental work (emeralds and rubies; gold plates with spiral patterns in gold wire; a cross encrusted with pearls).
Legend has it that this crown was a gift from the Byzantine Emperor Constantine IX Monomachus (1042–55) to Vladimir II Monomakh of Kiev (1113–25), but the dates alone make this impossible. The legend was evidently designed to establish the legitimacy of the Russian princes. The presentation of the Byzantine royal insignia (including the Cap of Monomakh) to the Grand Prince of Kiev is depicted on the sides of Ivan the Terrible's throne in the Cathedral of the Dormition.

Rooms 7 and 8

Saddles, bridles and other horse trappings from Russia (Tsar Mikhail Fyodorovich's saddle), the Caucasus, Central Asia, Europe, China, Iran and Turkey. Also of interest are the sleigh covers.

Room 9

One of the world's largest collections of State coaches: coach presented to Boris Godunov by Queen Elizabeth I; small coaches and sleighs made for the boy Peter I; the coronation coach of Tsaritsa Elizabeth; the summer coach of Catherine the Great; etc.

Diamond Fund (Almazny Fond)

A unique treasure-house (rarely open to the public): large lumps of gold, precious stones, jewellery and ornaments of exquisite beauty, etc.

First floor

Room 1

Arms and armour of the 13th–19th c.
Helmet of Grand Prince Yaroslav Vsevolodovich of Kiev (1238–46): conical in shape, with silver ornament (1216). The inscription states that the helmet belonged to Yaroslav, father of the famous Alexander Nevsky.
Helmet of Tsar Mikhail Romanov, the "Jericho Hat": gold on steel, 150 pearls, 152 precious stones (Moscow work, 1621). Also flintlocks, Western armour, the golden keys of the city of Riga, etc.

Room 2

Russian and Byzantine art: the Ryazan Hoard (12th–13th c.); gold cover of the icon of the Virgin of Vladimir (in Tretyakov Gallery – see entry); Gospel covers; goldsmiths' work, etc.

Room 3

Russian gold, silver and jewellery from 18th to early 20th c.

Room 4

Church vestments and secular costumes: vestments of Metropolitans Pyotr and Aleksey; robe belonging to Peter the Great; coronation robe of Catherine I, etc.

Room 5

Gifts from Poland, England (silver), Amsterdam (silver) and Germany.

Great Kremlin Palace (Bolskoy Kremlyovsky Dvorets)

Admission only with special permission

The Great Kremlin Palace was formerly the Tsar's Moscow residence. In addition to the Tsar's apartments, which have been left intact, it contains the assembly hall of the Supreme Soviet of the USSR and the Russian Soviet Federative Republic.
The palace, which has more than 700 rooms, was built for Tsar Nicholas I between 1838 and 1849 by Konstantin A. Thon and Nikolay A. Chichagov and associates. the main front facing the Moskva is 125 m (410 ft) long, in a style which harmonises with the Armoury and the Terem Palace. At first sight the building seems to have two storeys above the ground floor, but in fact there is only one upper storey with a double row of windows.

Ground floor

In the south wing of the ground floor are the former private apartments of the Tsar. The rather tasteless decoration and furnishings, left untouched after the Revolution for their historical interest, are a mixture of Late Rococo, Neo-classical, neo-Old Russian and other eclectic elements borrowed from the styles of the past.

Upper floor

The upper floor with its double row of windows contains the State apartments, named after various Russian orders, including St George's Hall (named after the Military Order of St

State coach in the Armoury Museum

Great Kremlin Palace and Ivan the Great Bell-Tower

Great Hall of the Palace of Facets

George, founded by Catherine II in 1769), a hall 61 m (200 ft) long by 20 m (65 ft) wide which is now mainly used for Government receptions.
St Andrew's Hall (the old Throne Room) and St Alexander's Hall were combined in 1933–34 (architect I. A. Ivanov-Shits) to form the Assembly Hall of the Supreme Soviet of the USSR and RSFSR. On the end wall of this large hall (seating for 3000), which is familiar to the Soviet public through its appearance in television news reports, is a monumental marble statue of Lenin.

Cathedral Square (Sobornaya Ploshchad)

Flanking this square in the centre of the Kremlin are the most important of its historic buildings – as the name of the square indicates, principally the cathedrals.
On the south side, adjoining the Great Kremlin Palace, is the Cathedral of the Annunciation. To the right (west) of this is the Cathedral of the Archangel Michael, the only one of the Kremlin cathedrals to have silver domes (though the central dome has recently been gilded). Next to this rises the Kremlin's tallest building, the Ivan the Great Bell-Tower, at the foot of which is the world's largest bell, the Emperor Bell.
On the north side of the square, set back a little, stands the former Patriarch's Palace with the Cathedral of the Twelve Apostles, now housing the Museum of 17th Century Folk Art and Culture. Between the Patriarch's Palace and the Bell-Tower is another great tourist attraction the Emperor Cannon (Tsar-Pushka).

Also on the north side of the square is the Cathedral of the Dormition, in which the Tsars were crowned. To the left of this, partly concealed, is the Church of the Deposition of the Robe. Between the Church of the Deposition of the Robe and the Palace of Facets to the west extends the east wall of the Terem Palace, with the cluster of golden domes belonging to the Tsar's domestic chapels (Upper Cathedral of the Saviour, Church of the Resurrection, Church of the Crucifixion).
Cathedral Square was originally formed at the beginning of the 14th c., in the reign of Ivan Kalita. Since the great building and rebuilding operations of 1475 to about 1530 it has been the central point of the Kremlin, and thus of Moscow.

**Cathedral of the Annunciation (Blagoveshchensky Sobor)

The Cathedral of the Annunciation with its nine gilded domes is the smallest of the three main Kremlin cathedrals, but the decoration of the interior (in particular the frescoes and icons by Andrey Rublyov and Feofan Grek) makes it one of the great treasures of Moscow.
The cathedral was built in 1484–89 by a team of builders from Pskov as the Court Church of Grand Prince Ivan III. It was connected by a passage at gallery level with the palace of the Grand Prince and later with the Tsar's residence. The passage still leads from the Gallery into the Great Kremlin Palace, which immediately adjoins the cathedral.
The nine domes and the arcade on the south side are reminiscent of the Cathedral of the Dormition in Vladimir, but there are also Renaissance features, since the Cathedral of the Annunciation was influenced by Aristotele Fioravanti's Cathedral of the Dormition, built only a short time earlier.

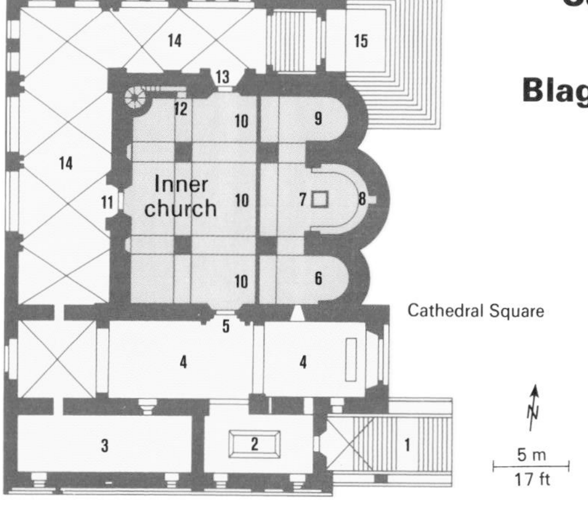

Cathedral of the Annunciation

Blagoveshchensky Sobor

1 Groznensky Steps
2 Reliquary
3 Sacristy
4 Parekklesion
5 South doorway
6 Diakonikon
7 High Altar
8 Bishop's throne
9 Prothesis
10 Iconostasis
11 West doorway
12 Up to choir
13 North doorway
14 Gallery
15 Steps to gallery

History

There were two earlier churches on the site – a 14th c. church on the foundations of which the present cathedral is built, and a slightly later one built between 1397 and 1416, during the reign of Vasily I, with paintings by Feofan Grek, Andrey Rublyov and Prokhor the Elder. This latter church, having become unsafe, was pulled down in 1482 and was replaced two years later by the present cathedral, built of brick on the high stone base of the earlier churches. It was in the form of a cube, with four pillars supporting the main dome and two domed apsidioles flanking the main apse. The church was surrounded by galleries – at first open but later given vaulted roofs – on the north, west and south sides.
After the 1547 fire Ivan the Terrible had the church restored and enlarged. Two "blind" domes were added flanking the main dome, and four small chapels with small domes and their own iconostases were built at gallery level, bringing the number of domes to nine. The domes were regilded in 1963.
In 1572, still in the reign of Ivan the Terrible, a further chapel was built at the south-east corner of the church and the steps leading up to the north-east entrance were constructed. In the 19th c. the sacristy was installed in the porch of the south-east chapel.

Interior

The visitor entering the Cathedral of the Annunciation is surprised by its small size, the space being still further reduced by the royal gallery at the west end, and by the paintings which cover every inch of the walls. The pavement of polished jasper dates from the reign of Ivan the Terrible.
Over the years the frescoes were frequently restored and overpainted, but during the thorough restoration of the church which was completed in 1961 the original layers of painting were exposed. An inscription records that the paintings were the work of Feodosy (Theodosius), son of Dionisy (Dionysius), and his assistants (1508). The finest of the frescoes are on the pillars, in the apse and diakonikon and on the gallery.

Iconostasis

The iconostasis is the icon-screen, with three doors, which separates the sanctuary of an Orthodox Church from the body of the church. In Russian Orthodox churches the iconostasis frequently reaches right up to the roof vaulting. The iconostasis originated as a simpler form of separation between the sanctuary and the rest of the church, with images on the beams of the architrave and curtains which later gave place to painted wooden panels. In Russia the iconostasis reached its full development at the end of the 14th c.
The iconostasis of the Cathedral of the Annunciation is the embodiment of a fully developed Russian iconostasis. According to the chronicler the paintings in the earlier church were by Feofan Grek, Andrey Rublyov and Prokhor the Elder; the chronicle also records that Rublyov's iconostasis was destroyed in the great fire of 21 June 1547. The restoration work revealed, however, that only some of the icons were damaged in the fire.
The iconostasis is divided vertically into the door level and four tiers above this – the *chin* (rank, dignity) tier; the festival tier; the tier of the Prophets; and the tier of the Patriarchs.

Door level:
There are three doors: the central or royal door, the north door to the left and the south door to the right.

Cathedral of the Annunciation ▶

The metal facing of the iconostasis (beaten bronze, gilded), including the ornamental mountings of the royal door and the base, are 19th c. work, to the design of Nikolay I. Sultanov.

Royal door:
The royal door, symbolising the gates of heaven, which led into the sanctuary could be used only by ordained priests and deacons. Formerly the (theocratic) Tsar was also allowed to pass through this door.
Between the royal door and the north door there was always an image of the Virgin. In this case it is the famous Virgin of the Don painted by Feofan Grek (copy; original in Tretyakov Gallery – see entry).
Between the royal door and the south door are a figure of the Saviour enthroned (1337) and a 17th c. copy of the Ustyug Annunciation (Tretyakov Gallery – see entry).

North and south doors:
The north and south doors lead into the two small rooms on either side of the sanctuary, the prothesis on the north side in which the bread and wine for the Eucharist were prepared and the diakonikon on the south side in which liturgical vestments, utensils and books were kept.

Chin (rank, dignity) tier:
Immediately above the doors is the principal tier of the iconostasis, the chin tier. The central group of icons on this tier is the Deesis or Intercession, with Christ as the Judge of the world enthroned in the centre and Mary (on left) and John the Baptist (on right) interceding for mankind. This, the basic Deesis, is here extended to include the Archangels Michael and Gabriel, the Apostles Peter and Paul and two Greek Fathers of the Church, Basil the Great and John Chrysostom.

Festival tier:
On this tier are fifteen icons of the annual Festivals of the Church. It was this tier that suffered most damage in the 1547 fire.

Tier of the Prophets:
In the centre of this tier is the Mother of God, with icons of the Prophets on either side. The icons were painted after the 1547 fire, probably by artists from Pskov.

Tier of the Patriarchs:
On the top tier, under ogee arches, are head-and-shoulder figures of the Old Testament Patriarchs, flanking a central icon of the Trinity. The icons are mostly 19th c.; one or two date from the 16th and 17th c.

*Palace of Facets (Granovitaya Palata)

Admission only with special permission

The Palace of Facets, built in 1487–91 by Marco Ruffo and Pietro Antonio Solari, is the only part of the huge complex constituted by the Great Kremlin Palace, the Terem Palace and associated buildings which has been almost completely preserved in its original form.

Façade

The name of the palace, which is almost exactly square in plan, comes from the faceted limestone blocks which pattern the main front – a form of rustication which originated in the Early Italian Renaissance.

The windows on the second floor, with rectangular framings in Naryshkin Baroque style and ornate columns borne on brackets, replaced the original twin pointed windows after a fire in 1682.

Interior

The interior of the palace can be seen only with special permission. Its principal features may be briefly mentioned.

Holy Vestibule:
The wall-paintings in the Holy Vestibule, the antechamber to the Great Hall, are 19th c. Two of the six doorways, decorated with carving and gilded, are false doors installed in the reign of Nicholas I.
The west doorway leads into St Vladimir's Hall in the Great Kremlin Palace.

Great Hall:
The historic old Great Hall, on a square plan with four low groined vaults borne on a single pier, creates a powerful impression by its size (just under 500 sq. m (5400 sq. ft)) and its magnificent wall-paintings. It served as a throne room and reception room. The original frescoes were destroyed in 1612, during the Polish occupation, and repainted in 1668 by Simon Ushakov. The present paintings were done in 1882 by two icon-painters from Palekh under the direction of the brothers Vladimir and Vasily Belusov, following detailed descriptions of the earlier frescoes by Ushakov himself. This restoration was necessary because the frescoes had been covered with whitewash in the 1670s and the walls hung with red velvet, following Western European models.

Palace of Facets, Great Kremlin Palace and Cathedral of the Annunciation (right to left)

The inner doorway, with carved decoration in Renaissance style, dates from the 15th and 16th c. The gilding of the carving and the ogee arch was carried out in the reign of Nicholas I; the canopy over the throne dates from the same period. (Photograph, p. 64).

** Terem Palace (Teremnoy Dvorets)

Admission only with special permission

A cluster of golden domes, glimpsed between the Palace of Facets and the Church of the Deposition of the Robe, is all that the ordinary visitor will see of this, the most splendid of the Kremlin's palaces.
In 1681–82 the Tsar's domestic chapels – the Upper Cathedral of the Saviour, the Church of the Crucifixion and the Church of the Resurrection – were given a common roof, out of which rise eleven gilded domes. The ornate crosses and the coloured tiles on the brick drums of the domes were designed by a woodcarver named Ippolit the Elder.
The interior of the Terem Palace – the finest example of Russian palace architecture of the first half of the 17th c. – can, like that of the Palace of Facets, be seen only with special permission.

History

The history of the building can be more easily followed on the south front (described below), which can only rarely be seen by visitors, than on the small section of the east side glimpsed between the Palace of Facets and the Church of the Deposition of the Robe. The following is a brief account.
The original Terem Palace was built by a team of architects (Antip Konstantinov, Bazhen Ogurtsov, Ivan Sharutin and others) in 1635–36 for Mikhail Fyodorovich, the first Romanov Tsar. There was much alteration and rebuilding in the 19th c., as a result of which only parts of the two long basement storeys survive from the original palace. Parts of the ground and first floors go back to Ivan III's palace, built by Aleviz Fryazin (Alevisio or Aloisio of Milan) in 1499–1508.
On these two basement storeys, set back, is the cube-shaped residential block, also of two storeys, with a flat roof surrounded by a balustrade which served as a terrace.
Above this again, set further back, is the Teremok, a tower or belvedere, with a hipped roof which was originally gilded. In this were the quarters of the royal children.

Golden Chamber of the Tsaritsa

In the basement storey on the east side of the palace is one of the few rooms to survive in its original state, the Golden Chamber of the Tsaritsa, named after its gilded decoration and wall-paintings. The vaulted ceiling of this room, in which the Tsaritsa used to receive high ecclesiastical and secular dignitaries, is borne on a single massive arch.
The wall-paintings which have been exposed since 1947 date from the late 16th c.: "Baptism of Grand Princess Olga", "Triumphal Procession of Tsaritsa Dinara after the Defeat of the Persians", etc.
The three east windows look out on the little square between the Palace of Facets and the Church of the Deposition of the Robe.

St Catherine's Church

On the north side of the Golden Chamber is St Catherine's Church, the Tsaritsa's domestic chapel, built by John Taylor in 1627. It was enclosed by other buildings and spoiled during the construction of the Great Kremlin Palace in 1838–49.

Façade of the Terem Palace

Interior of the Terem Palace: a palace of the "Arabian Nights"

Fairy-tale splendour in the royal apartments of the Terem Palace

Upper Cathedral of the Saviour

This church, above the Golden Chamber, was built in 1635–36 and served as the Tsar's domestic chapel.
The main features of interest are the iconostasis with its facing and royal door of beaten silver (1778) and the 17th c. icons. One of the icons is said to be an authentic portrait of Christ, "not made by the hand of man".

Stone Forecourt

Between the Upper Cathedral of the Saviour and the residential block is the Stone Forecourt. The staircase which descends from here to the Boyars' Square on the south side of the palace (the Lower Golden Staircase) is closed by a gilded copper grille (1670), decorated with a host of fabulous animals, long-tailed birds, horned heads, etc., within a pattern of spirals.

Church of the Crucifixion

The Upper Golden Staircase leads to the Church of the Crucifixion, built in 1681. It is notable particularly for the icons on the splendidly decorated iconostasis. Dating from soon after the building of the church, these are embroidered on silk, only the exposed parts of the body (face and hands) being painted in oil. Also of interest are the Crucifix by Ippolit the Elder (1687), a "Last Judgment" by Ivan A. Besmin, "St John the Theologian" by Ivan Y. Saltanov and a "Passion" from the Armoury workshops.

Church of the Resurrection

From the Church of the Crucifixion a richly decorated door leads into the Church of the Resurrection (1680–81), with a fine gilded iconostasis (about the turn of the 17th–18th c.).

South front

The churches described above and the Golden Chamber of the Tsaritsa lie behind the east wall of the Terem Palace, which can

be seen between the Palace of Facets and the Church of the Deposition of the Robe. Concealed behind the south front are the royal apartments, which can be seen only with special permission.
The south front is of fantastic effect with its squat pilaster-like features containing recesses and its double-arched windows topped by pediments (mostly broken) and richly carved limestone framings with a pendant between the arches ending in an animal's head.
In recesses in the cornice strip under the terrace balustrade are coloured tiles with coats of arms and plant and animal designs. The doorways of the Teremok are still more richly decorated: limestone arabesques with winged horses amid swirling foliage ornament, a pelican, winged Cupids armed with bows emerging from blossoms and shooting at birds, etc.

Royal apartments

The apartments on the third and fourth floors are reached from the Stone Forecourt by way of the Lower Golden Staircase. The five private apartments of the Tsars have low vaulted roofs with vaulted windows containing 19th c. stained glass which admits only a dim twilight. The interior appointments, painting and ornament combine to enhance the fairy-tale effect created by the south front. A visitor might well be forgiven for thinking that he had strayed into some Oriental palace from the "Arabian Nights."

Church of the Deposition of the Virgin's Robe (Tserkov Rizpolozheniya)

In front of the eleven domes of the Terem Palace is the Church of the Deposition of the Virgin's Robe, with a single dome. It was built in 1484–85 by the Pskov architects who were also responsible for the Cathedral of the Annunciation (1484–89). The church, which was linked by a staircase with the Patriarch's Palace, served as the domestic chapel of the Metropolitans and Patriarchs.

Exterior

The church is built on the foundations of an earlier church erected in 1451 and burned down in 1473. From Cathedral Square it is seen as a cubic structure on a high base. The three low projecting apses have blind arcading with ogee arches. Barrel vaults, also with ogee arches, form a transition to the dome, its tall drum resting on an octagonal base. The doorway on the south side, which is approached by a flight of steps, is framed in receding ogee arches.

Interior

The Church of the Deposition of the Robe is cruciform, with four pillars supporting the dome. The wall-paintings, which have been completely exposed only since the 1956 restoration, date from 1644 and are almost entirely on themes from the Acathist Hymn, a hymn of twenty-four verses in honour of the Virgin which is attributed to Romanus the Melodist, a hymnographer of the 5th/6th c.
The fine iconostasis (1627) is from the workshop of Nazary Istomin.

**Cathedral of the Dormition (Uspensky Sobor)

The Cathedral of the Dormition of the Virgin is the largest and most historic of the cathedrals in the Kremlin. Here Princes,

Grand Princes and Tsars were crowned by the Metropolitan or Patriarch, here Metropolitans and Patriarchs were enthroned and buried, and here many a chapter in the history of Moscow and of Russia began or was concluded. From its completion in 1479 until the 17th c. it provided an unmatchable model for all cathedral-building in Russia.
The Dormition (Falling Asleep or Death) of the Virgin, a festival celebrated by the Orthodox Church on 15 August, corresponds to the Roman Catholic festival of the Assumption, also celebrated on 15 August. The Cathedral of the Dormition is, therefore, sometimes referred to – wrongly – as the Cathedral of the Assumption.

History

In 1325/26 Pyotr, Metropolitan of Kiev and all Russia, moved his seat from Vladimir to Moscow, and in the same year Ivan I Kalita laid the foundation-stone of the Cathedral of the Dormition, Moscow's first stone church. It was consecrated on 4 August 1427.
In 1475–79 this church was replaced by a new Cathedral of the Dormition built by the Bologna architect Aristotele Fioravanti for Ivan III as a State church. This church has survived substantially in its original form (minor alterations to the façade after the 1547 fire and other small alterations to the interior in the mid 17th c.).

Kiev – Vladimir – Moscow:
While Fioravanti's cathedral provided a model for all later Russian cathedrals it was itself, according to the chroniclers, modelled on the Cathedral of the Dormition in Vladimir, which in turn had been built in 1158–61 in deliberate rivalry to the Cathedral of the Dormition in Kiev (1073–78). The historical background was as follows:
When, in 1299, Maksim, Metropolitan of Kiev and All Russia, moved his seat from Kiev to Vladimir on account of the Tatar menace, Vladimir inherited Kiev's role as the ecclesiastical centre of the Russian principalities.
During the reign of Metropolitan Pyotr (1307–26) contacts between the head of the church in Vladimir and the Moscow Princes and Grand Princes became increasingly close, and in 1325/26 the Metropolitan moved from Vladimir to Moscow. (Pyotr was subsequently – in 1339 – canonised). Moscow had thus succeeded Kiev and Vladimir as the seat of the Metropolitan, and its status as the political successor to Vladimir was finally established by Dmitry Donskoy's victory in the Battle of Kulikovo (1380).
But although Ivan Kalita built a Cathedral of the Dormition in the Kremlin immediately after the Metropolitan's move to Moscow this church still fell far short of the Vladimir Cathedral of the Dormition in magnificence and splendour. In order to remedy this Ivan III sent Aristotele Fioravanti to Vladimir, not so much to get ideas for his own new Cathedral of the Dormition as to have a standard of comparison which he could surpass by building a still more sumptuous cathedral.
The cathedral in the Kremlin admittedly owes a good deal to imitation but it owes much more to the consummate skill with which Fioravanti developed elements taken from Vladimir into something new and distinctive.

View from the south-east

The most striking view of the Cathedral of the Dormition is from the south-east. In spite of the cruciform plan which is revealed by the central dome and the four subsidiary domes, all gilded,

Church of the Deposition of the Robe

Cathedral of the Dormition

it is seen as a rectangular mass; the five low apses at the east end project only very slightly and do not detract from the compact effect; and the apses are rendered still more unobtrusive by the boldly projecting pilasters at the end of the east front and the greater projection of the round-headed gables (*zakomary*) on the east front as compared with those on the south front.

The cathedral, built of limestone and brick, stands on an unusually high base (4 m (13 ft); but compare the substructure of the Church of the Deposition to the rear), though this is largely concealed by the raising of the level of Cathedral Square.

The south front was the main front, with the main entrance (there are also doorways on the west end and the north side). The façade is vertically articulated by pilasters with imposts supporting the semicircular arches of the gables. Horizontally it is patterned by the base, a tier of blind arcading and a range of four slit windows like arrow-loops under the gables.

The arched south doorway is the finest of the cathedral's three doorways. It is decorated with frescoes which, like those on the west doorway, date from the 16th c. Painted on sheet copper in gold on a black ground, they depict Biblical scenes; above, the Virgin and Child.

Interior

The interior is of striking effect, thanks to its paintings but even more to its size and lightness. Compare the tiny Cathedral of the Annunciation, built by Russian architects, rendered still smaller by the royal gallery at the west end. In the Cathedral of the Dormition Fioravanti omitted the west gallery and created a spacious hall, with groined vaulting borne on four round piers (and four square pillars behind the iconostasis).

Cathedral of the Dormition
Uspensky Sobor

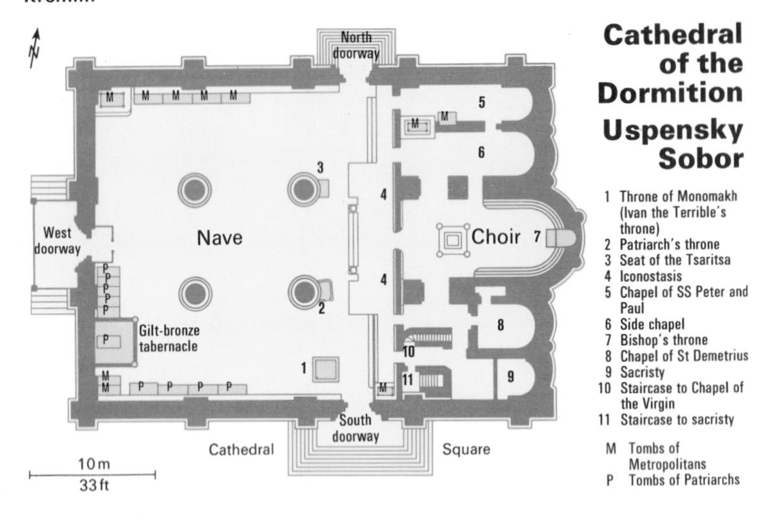

1 Throne of Monomakh (Ivan the Terrible's throne)
2 Patriarch's throne
3 Seat of the Tsaritsa
4 Iconostasis
5 Chapel of SS Peter and Paul
6 Side chapel
7 Bishop's throne
8 Chapel of St Demetrius
9 Sacristy
10 Staircase to Chapel of the Virgin
11 Staircase to sacristy

M Tombs of Metropolitans
P Tombs of Patriarchs

Ivan the Terrible's throne
To the left of the south doorway is the throne of Ivan the Terrible (1551), a magnificent example of Russian wood-carving. It is also known as the Throne of Monomakh, after the carvings on the sides depicting the presentation of the Byzantine imperial insignia by the Emperor Constantine IX Monomachus to Grand Prince Vladimir of Kiev, symbolising the transfer of Byzantine imperial authority to Russia. The presentation of the "Cap of Monomakh" (now in the Armoury) is also depicted.

Patriarch's throne
The richly decorated Patriarch's throne stands against the south-east pier.

Patriarchs' tombs
Along the north and south walls of the Cathedral are the tombs of Metropolitans and Patriarchs of the Russian Orthodox Church. The last Patriarch was Adrian (1690–1700), after whose death Peter the Great left the Patriarchal throne vacant, establishing instead (in 1721) the Holy Ruling Synod as the Church's highest authority. The Patriarchal constitution was restored by the Soviet Government, and on 5 November 1917 Tikhon, Metropolitan of Moscow, was chosen by lot to be Patriarch of the Russian Orthodox Church.

Tomb of Patriarch Hermogenes:
The gilt-bronze tabernacle in the south-west corner of the church, with a tent-roofed canopy borne on ogee arches, contains the sarcophagus of Patriarch Germogen or Hermogenes (1606–12). Hermogenes had excommunicated the

Interior of the Cathedral of the Dormiton ▶

Polish invaders of Russia, and during the Polish occupation of Moscow, in 1612, he was imprisoned by the Poles and starved to death. After his death the Patriarchal throne was left vacant for Filaret, a member of the Romanov family, who in 1608 had set up as a rival Patriarch under the second False Dmitry and in 1619 was officially enthroned as Patriarch, assuming the style of Veliky Gosudar (Great Sovereign), hitherto reserved for the Tsar.

Frescoes

The frescoes of 1642–43 underwent extensive restoration between 1911 and 1960. The earliest frescoes in the church were painted by Dionisy in the 1480s; then in 1513–15, when they were already in poor condition, they were overpainted; and finally in 1642–43 more than a hundred icon-painters from all over Russia took part in the third painting of the church, carefully following the originals. In 1773 the frescoes were overpainted in oils, and further overpainting was carried out in the reign of Nicholas I.

Iconostasis

In 1812 the cathedral was occupied by Napoleon's Grand Army. The icons were used as firewood, and some 250 kg (550 lb) of gold and 5 tons of silver were carried off. Most of this booty was abandoned during the French army's retreat and was recovered and returned to the cathedral.
The 16 m (52 ft) high iconostasis dates from 1652; the silver-gilt frame is 19th c. Most of the icons are copies (originals in the Tretyakov Gallery, see entry), but a few, particularly on the lowest tier, are original.
At door level are icons of the "Saviour with the Fiery Eye" (14th c.), the "Dormition" and the "Old Testament Trinity" (16th c.; head of right-hand angel 14th c.).
To the left of the royal door is the famous "Virgin of Vladimir" (a 17th c. copy; original in Tretyakov Gallery).
Other fine icons are those of Metropolitan Peter, with sixteen scenes from his life (*c.* 1480), St George (12th c.) and St Alexius the Man of God.

Patriarch's Palace, with the Cathedral of the Twelve Apostles and the Museum of 17th Century Russian Art and Culture

The three-storey palace of the reforming Patriarch Nikon, with the Cathedral of the Twelve Apostles which served as his private chapel, now houses the Museum of 17th Century Russian Art and Culture. Erected in 1653–56, the building reflects Nikon's objection to the tent roof as reminiscent of secular building and his dislike of the Old Russian or "fairy-tale" style: like the Cathedral of the Dormition, it is a compact mass on a high base, with a cruciform plan and five domes.

Museum

Room 1 (Hall of the Cross):
The principal attraction is the Hall of the Cross, a vaulted hall with an area of 250 sq. m (2700 sq. ft), its roof supported without the use of columns. This was the meeting-place of Church Synods and the scene of State receptions. When the Patriarchate was replaced by the Holy Ruling Synod in the reign of Peter the Great the palace was occupied by monks, who produced the consecrated oil in the Hall of the Cross.
A prominent feature of the room is the stove (1675–80) used in the preparation of the consecrated oil. Another interesting item

The world's largest cannon, the Emperor Cannon

The Emperor Bell

Ivan the Great Bell-Tower

is the silver basin (1767) in which the oil was kept. Notable among the other exhibits are Russian and Western European silver (silver chess set, 17th c. silver globe from Augsburg), Oriental fabrics and Russian pearl embroidery.

Room 2:
Arms and armour.

Room 3:
Gold liturgical utensils.

Rooms 4 and 5:
Tiled ovens, domestic equipment, etc.

Room 6:
Iconostasis from the Monastery of the Ascension (demolished after the October Revolution); icons, vestments, etc.

*Emperor Cannon (Tsar Pushka)

The Emperor Cannon is the world's largest cannon, with a calibre of 890 mm (35 in), 5·34 m (17½ ft) long and weighing 40 tonnes, it was cast in 1586 by Andrey Shchokhov. On the barrel is a likeness of Tsar Fyodor I Ivanovich.

*Emperor Bell (Tsar Kolokol)

At the foot of the Ivan the Great Bell-Tower, on a granite base (designed by the Neo-classical French architect Auguste-Richard Montferrand, who did most of his work in St Petersburg), is the world's largest bell, the 210 tonne Emperor Bell. It stands 6·14 m (20 ft) high and has a diameter at the base of 6·60 m (22 ft). Even the small piece which broke off during a fire in 1737 weighs 11·5 tonnes.
The Bell was cast by Ivan and Mikhail Motorin in 1734–35, during the reign of the Empress Anna Ivanova. It consists of just under 80 per cent copper. It is decorated in relief with portraits of the second Romanov Tsar, Aleksey Mikhailovich, and the Empress Anna Ivanovna, five icons and two inscriptions.

*Ivan the Great Bell-Tower (Kolokolnya Ivan Veliky)

The Ivan the Great Bell-Tower is the tallest structure in the Kremlin (81 m (266 ft)), and until the end of the Second World War it was the tallest in Moscow. Unlike the other Kremlin towers, now topped by the Soviet star, Ivan the Great has retained its original cross.
From the top of the tower, which was increased in height by Boris Godunov in 1600, making it the tallest tower in Russia, the view extends for some 40 km (25 miles). There are 329 steps to the top.

History

The site of the present complex consisting of the Bell-Tower, the Belfry and the Filaret Building was originally occupied by an early 14th c. church built in the reign of Ivan I Kalita and dedicated to St John Climacus (*c.* 579–649), a hermit who became Abbot of St Catherine's Monastery on Sinai and wrote a celebrated treatise, the "Ladder of Paradise" ("Klimax tou Paradisou").

Cathedral of the Archangel Michael

The domes of the Archangel Cathedral

This church was replaced in 1505–08 by a two-storey church built by Bon Fryazin (Marco Bono), also dedicated to St John (Ivan) Climacus. The tower was built at the same time; an additional storey was added in the reign of Boris Godunov.

Exterior

The tower, built of brick, stands on a base of white dressed stone. Successive storeys, octagonal in plan, decrease in size, ending in platforms with arched openings for the bells. The top section, with the dome and its summit cross, was added in 1600, as a three-part inscription (regilded in 1967) records: "By the grace of the Holy Trinity and on the order of Tsar and Grand Prince Boris Fyodorovich, autocrat of All Russia, and his Orthodox son Fyodor Borisovich, Tsarevich of All Russia, this sacred place was completed and gilded in the second year of their reign."

Belfry

The Belfry, next to the Bell-Tower, was built between 1532 and 1543 by an Italian architect known as Petrok Maly. The Renaissance features in the lowest storey on the side facing Cathedral Square are unmistakable. In the arched openings hang the bells, the heaviest of which is the 19th c. Dormition Bell (65·5 tonnes).

Filaret Building

The third element in the complex, also with a tower and arched openings for bells, was built in 1624 during the reign of the Romanov Patriarch Filaret whose name it bears.

**Cathedral of the Archangel Michael (Arkhangelsky Sobor)

The Cathedral of the Archangel Michael, built in 1505–08 by Alevisio the Younger, was the burial church of the Tsars. Here

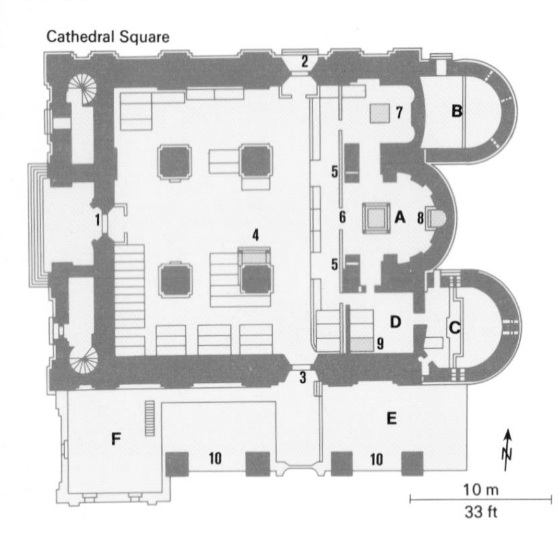

Cathedral of the Archangel

Arkhangelsky Sobor

A Chapel of the Archangel Michael (altars)
B Chapel of St Varus
C Chapel of John the Baptist
D Diakonikon
E Sacristy
F Tent-roofed annexe (19th c.)

1 West doorway
2 North doorway
3 South doorway
4 Reliquary of Tsarevich Dmitry Ivanovich
5 Iconostasis
6 Royal door
7 Altar of Offerings
8 Bishop's throne
9 Tomb of Ivan the Terrible
10 Buttresses

all the Princes, Grand Princes and Tsars from Ivan Kalita onwards had their last resting-place, with the exception of Boris Godunov, who, with his wife, is buried in the Monastery of the Trinity at Zagorsk (see Practical Information – Excursions).

After St Petersburg became the capital in 1712 the Tsars and Emperors from Peter the Great onwards were buried in the cathedral in the Peter and Paul Fortress; the exception was Peter II, who died of smallpox in Moscow in 1730.

History

The present church was built on the foundations of an earlier church built by Ivan Kalita in 1333 in thanksgiving for relief from famine. The original church had frescoes (not preserved) painted by Feofan Grek (Theophanes the Greek) in 1399.

The demolition of the first Cathedral of the Archangel began on 21 May 1505, and the new one built by Alevisio the Younger was consecrated on 8 November 1508: a rectangular structure with a system of five domes displaced towards the east end. The two slightly smaller domes are over the lateral apses. Unlike the other Kremlin cathedrals, the Cathedral of the Archangel has silver domes, apart from the recently gilded central dome. The cathedral was surrounded on three sides by galleries, which were demolished in the 18th c. with the exception of part of the south gallery. The tent-roofed annexe at the south-west corner was built in 1826, and the buttresses on the south side were also later additions. The two single-domed chapels beyond the north and south apses date from the mid 16th c. The cathedral was thoroughly restored in 1955.

Exterior

The façade, like that of the Cathedral of the Dormition, is divided by pilasters topped by imposts bearing the rounded gables. The five vertical divisions of the north front are of different widths, corresponding to the various elements in the plan.

Iconostasis, Cathedral of the Archangel (detail) ▶

The narrow west work contained the Chapel of St Aquila, with windows opening into the nave, which was originally reserved for the ladies of the royal family.
At the east end is the section containing the sanctuary and apses. On the north side is the Chapel of St Varus, a tiny structure with a single dome.
Horizontally the building is articulated by an ornamental freize half-way up the wall, with blind arcading below this and above it a series of blind recesses and – the most striking feature of all – scallop-shells under the gable arches.

Interior

The interior appears very narrow, with square pillars breaking it up into three barrel-vaulted aisles. The most notable features are the royal tombs, the frescoes and the iconostasis.

Tombs

The forty-eight brick sarcophagi (some of which are double) contain the remains of fifty-four Princes, Grand Princes and Tsars and some of their sons; they all date from 1636–37. The uniform bronze covers were added in 1903, during the reign of the last Tsar, Nicholas II. The finest tombs are those of Tsarevich Dmitry and Ivan the Terrible.

Reliquary of Dmitry Ivanovich:
On the north side of the south-east pier is the Reliquary of Dmitry Ivanovich (murdered in 1591), of limestone, partly gilded, which dates from 1638. The silver plate with scenes from Dmitry's life which formerly covered the reliquary is now in the Armoury.
Dmitry was killed at Uglich in 1591, when he was eight years old, in circumstances which remain mysterious. Popular opinion blamed Boris Godunov for his death. During the Time of Troubles a number of "False Dmitrys" came forward, each claiming that he was legitimate heir to the throne who had escaped Boris Godunov's attempt on his life. The best known of the pretenders were the first two, known as Pseudo-Demetrius I and II.
The remains of the murdered Prince were transferred to the Cathedral of the Archangel in 1606 by Tsar Vasily IV Shuisky, and thereafter were revered as wonder-working.

Frescoes

Of the frescoes painted by Feofan Grek in the earlier cathedral in 1399 nothing survives. The early 16th c. frescoes of the new cathedral were removed a century later and replaced by new ones. The sequence of the original frescoes was recorded before they were destroyed, and although the new paintings followed the same pattern they were very different in style. Among the painters who contributed to the 17th c. decoration was Simon Ushakov.
These frescoes were completely overpainted in the 18th and 19th c., and were not exposed in their original form until the second half of the 20th c.
North and south walls: scenes featuring the Archangel Michael and Old Testament scenes; below, New Testament scenes and legends of the Emperor Constantine.
West Wall: Last Judgement.
Royal portraits: The lower part of the walls of the Burial Vault has more than sixty portraits of Princes, Grand Princes and Tsars, with the name of the patron saint below each one. Many of them are copies: originals in the Tretyakov Gallery (see entry).

Palace of Congresses

Trinity Tower

Iconostasis

The iconostasis (1680–81) was the work of a group of artists under the direction of Ivan Nedumov. The icons were restored and the richly decorated royal door was installed in the early 19th c.
The icon of the Archangel Michael, with eighteen scenes from his legend in panels round the sides, dates from the turn of the 14th–15th c.

Palace of Congresses (Dvorets Syezdov)

Admission only with special permission

The Palace of Congresses, built in 1960–61 by a team of artists led by M. V. Posokhin, is the most modern building within the precincts of the Kremlin – a structure of triangular marble pylons and gleaming glass.
The architects were awarded the Lenin Prize in 1962, and the Palace of Congresses became the model for modern Soviet urban architecture. The objective of the planners was to create a building which would be in harmony with the late medieval façades of the cathedrals and towers; and accordingly the permitted height of the building, which was the subject of an architectural competition, was restricted, so that much of the accommodation is underground. But at the same time the building – erected within the Kremlin precincts, which until 1958 had been almost sacrosanct – was to be open to all.
The Palace of Congresses is, therefore, also designed as a theatre and public hall, used for congresses, ceremonial occasions, performances by the Bolshoy Company, film festivals and political rallies as well as meetings of the Communist Party of the Soviet Union.

Captured French cannon in front of the Arsenal

The main auditorium is the largest in the Soviet Union – 50 m (165 ft) long and 20 m (65 ft) high, with seating for 6000. It is equipped with 7000 concealed loudspeakers and has excellent acoustics.
Escalators lead up to the Banqueting Hall, in which refreshments are served during the intervals in performances and which affords magnificent views of the Kremlin and of Moscow.
Although admission to the Palace of Congresses is normally possible only with special permission, visitors can, of course, see it on evenings when there is a public performance of some kind.

Trinity Tower (Troitskaya Bashnya)

Opening times
Daily 10 a.m.–7 p.m.

Between the Palace of Congresses and the Arsenal is the massive Trinity Gate-Tower, which gives access to Manezh Street (Manezhnaya Ulitsa), also to the Alexander Garden and the Lenin Library (see entries). It is linked with the Kutafya Tower by the Trinity Bridge.
The seven-storey Trinity Tower, the tallest of the Kremlin towers and the counterpart on the west side of the Saviour's Tower (see Red Square) on the east, was built in 1495. The superstructure with its octagonal tent roof dates from 1685, when almost all the Kremlin towers were given their present roofs.

Kutafya Tower

The Kutafya Tower is reached from the Trinity Tower on the Trinity Bridge, built in 1516 over the Neglinnaya (now flowing

Council of Ministers Building, formerly the Senate

underground), which then served as a moat; the bridge was renovated in 1901.
The Kutafya Tower was built about the same time as the bridge to protect the river crossing. Like many other Kremlin towers, it was given a new superstructure in 1685, in this case a balustraded wall of open windows.

Arsenal

Admission only with special permission

The Arsenal was built between 1702 and 1736, with some interruptions to the work, on the site of the Granary, which was burned down in 1701. The general plan of the building was sketched out by Peter the Great himself; the architects were Dmitry Ivanov, Christoph Konrad and others.
It was given its present aspect between 1815 and 1828, after the French attempts to blow up the Kremlin before abandoning Moscow had made radical rebuilding neccessary. The work was begun under the direction of Osip I. Bove, who erected a plain Neo-classical building, with wings laid out in trapezoid form round a pentagonal central courtyard. The Baroque portico was added by Dmitry V. Ukhtomsky.
After the rebuilding it was intended to use the Arsenal as an army museum: hence the 875 cannon lining the outside walls. The stucco reliefs of military trophies on the walls reflect the same intention.
The tower to the north of the Arsenal is the Corner Arsenal Tower, which can be seen better from the Tomb of the Unknown Soldier in the Alexander Garden (see entry).

For the tower to the north-west of the Arsenal, the Middle Arsenal Tower, also see Alexander Garden.
The tower immediately east of the main front of the Arsenal is St Nicholas's Tower (see Red Square).

Council of Ministers Building

Admission only with special permission

The Council of Ministers Building, formerly the Senate and from 1918 the seat of the Soviet Government, is a prominent landmark with its huge green dome topped by the national flag. The Senate was built between 1776 and 1788 to the design of Matvey F. Kazakov. A portico in the form of a triumphal arch, with four Ionic columns and a pediment, leads into the inner courtyard, which is divided into three sections by two transverse wings. The main front, set on a high base, has rusticated masonry on the ground floor and Doric pilasters on the two upper floors.

Sverdlov Hall

Directly under the dome, at the apex of the triangle formed by the three main wings of the building, is the Sverdlov Hall, one of the finest halls in Moscow, in which the Central Committee of the Communist Party of the Soviet Union meets.
Round this circular hall, 25 m (80 ft) in diameter and 27 m (90 ft) high, are closely set Corinthian columns, between which are allegorical reliefs depicting Justice, Philanthropy, Law-abidingness, etc. (copies: originals in the Armoury). Higher up are reliefs of Russian Grand Princes and Tsars, the originals of which are also in the Armoury.

Saviour's Tower

Statue of Lenin

Secret Tower and First Nameless Tower; to rear Ivan the Great Bell-Tower

Lenin's Flat

In the east wing are the two rooms (seen only with special permission) occupied by Lenin and his wife from 1918 to 1922. Reproductions of the rooms, particularly of the one which served both as study and as bedroom, are to be seen in almost all the Soviet Union's Lenin Museums (see Practical Information – Museums).

Senate Towers

Behind the Council of Ministers Building is the Senate Tower (see Red Square).

Presidium of the Supreme Soviet of the USSR/Kremlin Theatre

Admission only with special permission

The Neo-classical building beside the Saviour's Gate houses the Presidium of the Supreme Soviet of the USSR and the Kremlin Theatre.
The building was erected in 1932–34 for use as Government offices. The Kremlin Theatre, which has the most modern equipment and seating for 1200, was opened in 1958 with a performance of a play featuring Lenin, "Bells of the Kremlin". The theatre is principally used for performances by visiting companies from all over the Soviet Union.
Although the Presidium building can normally be seen only with special permission the public are of course admitted to performances in the theatre.

Lenin Monument

On the south-east side of the Presidium building is the spacious Kremlin Square, in which, on the edge of the Tainitsky Garden to the south, is a statue of Lenin by the contemporary sculptor Pintsuk (1967).

The Saviour's Tower adjoining the Presidium building and its neighbours the Tsar's Tower, Alarm Tower, Constantine and Helen Tower and Beklemishev Tower are described in the entry for Red Square.

Towers on the south side of the Kremlin

The towers along the Moskva side of the Kremlin can be seen from the Tainitsky Garden inside the walls or from the Kremlin Embankment (Kremlyovskaya Naberezhnaya) outside the walls.
The Beklemishev Tower at the east end of the south side is described under Red Square.

St Peter's Tower

St Peter's Tower (Petrovskaya Bashnya), built about 1500, is named after the first Metropolitan of Moscow, Peter, who was later canonised. It was frequently destroyed in the course of its history – in 1612 by the Poles, in the reign of Catherine II in preparation for the planned rebuilding of the Kremlin, in 1812 by the French – but each time was rebuilt.

Second Nameless Tower

The Second Nameless Tower (Vtoraya Bezymyannaya Bashnya) – its official name! – was built about 1500 and has been preserved substantially in its original form.
The octagaonal tent-roofed superstructure dates, like the superstructures of other towers, from 1680.

First Nameless Tower

The First Nameless Tower (Pervaya Bezymyannaya Bashnya) was also built about 1500. In the reign of Ivan IV it was used for

River front of the Kremlin: Water Tower, Great Kremlin Palace and Cathedral of the Archangel

storing powder. An explosion in the powder magazine caused heavy damage, and the tower was pulled down under Catherine II's plan for rebuilding the Kremlin. After being rebuilt it was blown up by the French in 1812 and was again rebuilt by Osip I. Bove on the basis of old sketches and plans.

Secret Tower

The Secret Tower (Taynitskaya Bashnya) is named after a secret underground passage leading out of the Kremlin. It was the first of the Kremlin towers, built by Pietro Antonio Solari in 1485. It was demolished in preparation for Catherine II's planned (but never executed) rebuilding of the Kremlin, and was rebuilt by Osip I. Bove in 1817–19, broadly in its original form. It was originally a gate-tower, but the gateway was walled up in 1930.

Annunciation Tower

The Annunciation Tower (Blagoveshchenskaya Bashnya) was built in 1487–88, the superstructure about 1700.

The name of the tower comes from an icon of the Annunciation which was once displayed on the tower. (Many of the Kremlin towers are named after monasteries which no longer exist but were once connected with the Kremlin by a road running from one of the towers. The name of the monastry was given to the road and to the tower, and an icon of the appropriate saint or festival was set up in the gateway of the tower.)

Water Tower

The Water Tower (Vodovzvodnaya Bashnya), like the other corner towers, is circular so that its guns could cover the whole field of fire. It was built in 1488 by Anton Fryazin ("Fryazin" being the term applied to Italians or "Franks"). The tower acquired its present name in 1633, when a pump was installed in it to being up water from the Moskva to water the Kremlin gardens. It was badly damaged in 1812 when the French tried to blow it up, but was rebuilt in 1817 by Osip I. Bove.

Lenin Library/Pashkov House

(Biblioteka imeni Lenina, Dom Pashkova)

H12

Location
3 Kalinin Avenue
(Prospekt Kalinina 3)

Metro
Biblioteka im. Lenina

The imposing Lenin Library, of which the Pashkov House forms part, is the largest library in Europe, with 29 million volumes, and one of the largest and most modern libraries in the world. This gigantic complex, with five library buildings, occupies the whole of a city block. Designed by Vladimir A. Shchuko and V. G. Helfreich, it was built between 1928 and 1940, though the interior was not completed until 1958.

Particularly impressive are the façades looking towards the Kremlin (see entry) and the Central Exhibition Hall, notably the main entrance with its Neo-classical granite-clad colonnades. Note also the rich sculptural decoration of the two attic friezes, the allegorical figures, busts and portrait medallions. The leading Soviet sculptors of the day and contributed to the decoration of both the exterior and the interior.

Pashkov House

The Pashkov House, a mansion in Early Neo-classical style, stands on higher ground behind the Lenin Library, into which it was incorporated in 1940.

This palatial residence, consisting of a central block and two

The Neo-classical Pashkov House, now part of the Lenin Library

symmetrical wings linked with it by galleries, was built in 1784–86. The façades of the wings have four Ionic columns, while the main building, which stands higher, is preceded by a Corinthian portico. The whole complex is dominated by a circular belvedere.

Lenin Mausoleum

See Red Square

Lenin Museum

See Central Lenin Museum

Lenin Stadium

See Luzhniki Sports Complex

Lomonosov University

D7

Metro
Universitet

South-west of the Moskva, which here describes a wide bend round the Luzhniki Sports Complex (see entry), is the main

The Lenin Stadium in the Luzhniki Sports Complex

building of Moscow's Lomonosov University, the largest university in the Soviet Union, founded in 1755. This massive skyscraper (1949–53), 240 m (790 ft) and twenty-eight storeys high, contains the University's teaching and research departments; the flanking wings are students' residences.
The University's Gorky Library has a stock of some 6 million volumes.

Luzhniki Sports Complex E8/9, F8

The Luzhniki Sports Complex, an extensive area with a number of halls and stadiums, lies in a wide bend of the River Moskva. Many events in the 22nd Summer Olympic Games in 1980 took place here.

Metro
Sportivnaya

Lenin Stadium

In the centre of the area is the immense Lenin Stadium, originally built in 1955 and overhauled for the 1980 Olympics (floodlighting installation). The stadium can accommodate more than 100,000 spectators, most of them in the open.

Palace of Sport and Little Arena

The Palace of Sport and Little Arena lie north-west of the Lenin Stadium. The Palace of Sport, which can seat 12,000 spectators, is designed to accommodate a variety of sports; it can be flooded to form an ice-rink.
The Little Arena has seating for 10,000 spectators.

Swimming Stadium and Friendship Hall

Like many other sports facilities in Moscow, the Swimming Stadium was thoroughly renovated for the 1980 Olympics.

Entrance to the Kropotkinskaya Metro station

Immediately adjoining it is the Friendship Hall, one of the few entirely new buildings erected for the Olympics. Its concrete dome with triangular window openings looks like the shell of a large tortoise.
The Olympic Village was built some distance away to the south-west, beyond Lomonosov University (see entry). The other stadiums housing Olympic events were widely scattered within the city.

*Metro stations

Services in operation
Daily 6 a.m.–1 a.m.,
public holidays 6 a.m.–2 a.m.

When Moscow's first Metro line, 11·2 km (7 miles) long, with thirteen stations, opened on 15 May 1935 passengers found themselves in surroundings very different from other buildings in the capital – palatial stations, spacious halls with chandeliers, huge concourses decorated with mosaics, constructed by an army of workers, artists and engineers under the direction of Nikita S. Khrushchov, then the city's Party Chief, with a lavish use of 70,000 sq. m (750,000 sq. ft) of multi-coloured marble, precious metals, bronze, mosaics, gold and glass.
These first stations, planned by Stalin as prestige and show buildings, set a standard which the designers of subsequent stations sought to maintain. Although the sumptuous decoration of Stalinist times is no longer in favour, Moscow's Metro must still be the most luxurious underground railway system in the world.
Thus the flat-rate fare of 5 copecks not only covers a journey of any length (see Practical Information – Public Transport) but

Komsomolskaya Metro station: a palace of marble, stucco and gold

also gives admission to a whole series of unique underground museums. While in most cities the underground system aims only to achieve functional efficiency, the Moscow underground stations meet two requirements: they are functional, but they also offer art for the enjoyment of passengers. The decoration of each station is related to a different theme.

Even visitors who do not need to use the Metro system for transport should at least look into one or two of the principal stations. Any time is suitable apart from the rush hours (7–9 a.m. and 4–6 p.m.).

Since the Metro operates until after midnight and most restaurants close at eleven o'clock, a sightseeing trip to some of these underground "museums" offers an alternative to the night life which is hard to find in Moscow.

Visitors need have no fear for their safety in using the Metro at night – unlike some other cities in both East and West.

Komsomolskaya

Perhaps the most impressive station is Komsomolskaya, in Komsomol Square (Komsomolskaya Ploshchad), which also has the Leningrad, Yaroslavl (see entry) and Kazan railway stations. Constructed in 1952, it is named after the Communist League of Youth (Komsomol) founded in 1918.

The main concourse has seventy-two octagonal marble-clad piers supporting small round arches. The central section is dominated by huge chandeliers suspended from the highest point of decorative but non-functional stucco ribs. Between the chandeliers are eight monumental mosaics framed in elaborate stucco mouldings depicting scenes from Russian history.

Kievskaya

The Kievskaya Metro station, beneath the Kiev railway station, dates from the Stalin period. In addition to mosaics and chandeliers it is notable for its arcades with sculptural decoration.

Mayakovskaya

The Mayakovskaya Station (1938–39), named after the poet Vladimir Mayakovsky (1893–1930), is notable for its sense of vertical space and its indirectly lit dome mosaics. The lateral arcades and the main arches are supported on stainless-steel pillars. The mosaics, in fluorescent materials, were designed by Aleksandr A. Deineka, an exponent of Socialist Realism (see Tretyakov Gallery, Rooms 40–52); the twenty-five scenes, one in each bay, depict the Soviet conquest of space.
On 6 November 1941, when a state of siege had been declared in Moscow and the Germans were within 10 km (6 miles) of the capital, Stalin made a famous speech to the Supreme Soviet, meeting in the station.

Novoslobodskaya

The main attraction of the Novoslobodskaya Station (1952) is its stained glass, with variations on themes from Russian tapestries – vases, rosettes, plants, figures, etc.

Ploshchad Revolutsii

This station (1939) in Revolution Square (Ploshchad Revolutsii), conveniently situated for the Central Lenin Museum, Red Square and the Kremlin (see entries), appropriately takes the October Revolution as its theme. Under its forty arches are bronze figures, in pairs, of "Heroes of the Revolution" – idealised representations of those who made the Revolution possible and contributed to the building up of the Soviet State. Among them are a kneeling Young Pioneer with his gun slung round his neck; the crew of the cruiser "Aurora"; a frontier guard and his dog, with ears pricked expectantly; a mother and child; and various sportsmen (footballers, a girl discus-thrower). Each figure – whether an architect bent over his plans or a young girl reading – is represented in a typical but idealised manner.

Ploshchad Sverdlova

The Ploshchad Sverdlova (Sverdlov Square) Station, in the city centre, is devoted to the art of the Soviet peoples.

Other stations

Other stations of the Stalin era which are worth seeing include Kropotinskaya, Biblioteka imeni Lenina, Prospekt Marksa, Lermontovskaya and Paveletskaya. There are also a number of notable newer stations such as Leninskie Gory (1959).

Metro Museum

In the Sportivnaya Station is the Museum on the History of the Metro (Muzey Istorii Metropolitena).

Museum on the History and Reconstruction of Moscow

(Muzey Istorii i Rekonstruktsii Moskvy) **K13 (E1)**

Location
12 New Square
(Novaya Ploshchad 12)

Metro
Dzerzhinskaya

The Museum on the History and Reconstruction of Moscow is housed in the Neo-classical Church of St John the Evangelist (1825). A visitor who, after seeing the exterior of the church, goes through the two sections of the museum, devoted to Moscow before and after the Revolution, may be led to speculate on the symbolic character of the association between history, reconstruction, revolution and the church.

Museum on the History of Moscow

Novodevichy Convent

With its large collection of archaeological finds, old prints, pictures, town plans, views, models and photographs, the museum is focused on a number of main themes: the earliest settlements on the Kremlin hill, the burning of Moscow in 1812, the replanning and rebuilding after the fire, the October Revolution, the Great Fatherland War of 1941–45, developments since the war and building plans up to the year 2000.

**Novodevichy Convent (Novodevichy Monastyr) E9

Location
Novodevichy Passage (Novodevichy Proezd)

Metro
Sportivnaya

Opening times
Wed.–Mon. 10 a.m.–5.30 p.m.

Closed
Tues. and last day of month

The Novodevichy Convent (New Convent of the Maidens), situated in a loop of the Moskva, is one of the finest and most interesting of Moscow's old religious houses. Seen from some distance away, with its fifteen buildings of the 16th and 17th c, it looks more like a fairy-tale city than a convent. It was converted into a museum of architecture in 1922, and became a branch of the Historical Museum (see entry) in 1934.
Numbers of artists set up their easels in the arcades at the entrance, and visitors may be tempted by the opportunity of picking up a "home-made" souvenir of their visit. The prices asked for water-colours and sketches are relatively low; but, since the artists are at their posts even in sharp frost, the trade seems to be profitable.

History

The convent was founded by Vasily III in 1514 to commemorate the capture of Smolensk and was designed to form part of the ring of fortified monasteries round Moscow. As in the case of the Don Monastery (see entry), however, only the principal

Novodevichy Convent
Novidevichy Monastyr

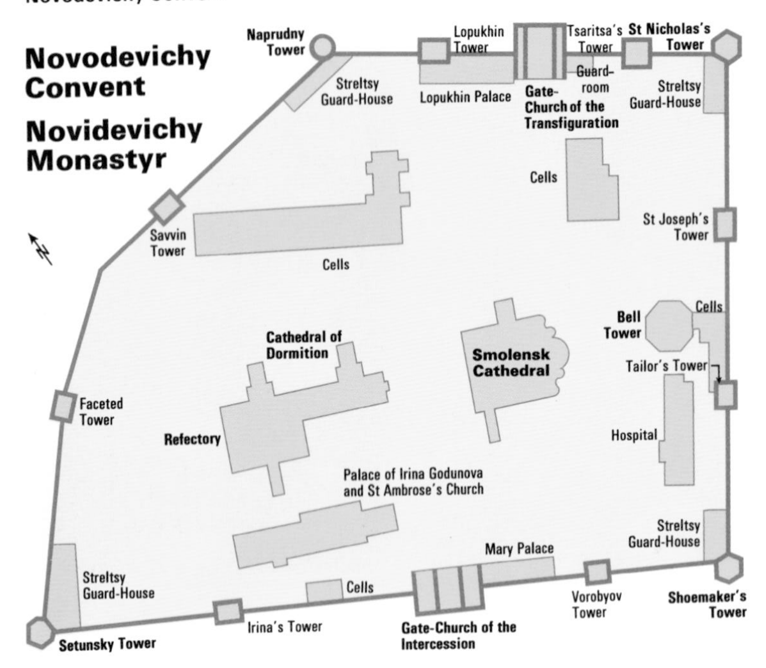

cathedral was built in the first place. This was the Smolensk Cathedral (1524–25), the only early 16th c. building in the complex. The walls and towers were built at the end of the 16th c., following the model of the Kremlin walls, but by then the time for such defensive structures was almost over.

The heyday of the convent was in the 17th and 18th c., particularly during the Regency (1682–89) of Sophia, Peter the Great's half-sister. The "maidens" of the convent – often ladies who were considered by the rulers of the day to be too dangerous or influential – mostly belonged to the higher ranks of society, and although they were prisoners in the convent were generously supplied with money by their noble relatives. The convent was thus able to carry out an active building programme, in the Moscow Baroque manner rather than the Old Russian style.

For many years now the convent has been in course of restoration, and only a few of the buildings are open to the public. Even the cemetery, with the graves of Chekhov, Gogol and other notable people, is likely to remain closed for some time. The convent is still well worth a visit, however, for the sake of the fantastic exterior views and the interior of the Smolensk Cathedral.

Smolensk Cathedral

The finest building in the Novodevichy Convent is the Smolensk Cathedral, which has been open to the public for some years. Externally it is very similar to the Cathedral of the Dormition in the Kremlin (see entry), on which it is modelled.

Polytechnic Museum

Its main attraction, however, is the interior with its frescoes, icons and magnificent iconostasis.
The frescoes (1526–30) are primarily representations of religious themes, but their symbolism goes beyond the religious message to express the Russian State's sense of triumph after the conquest of Smolensk, and they are thus of great historical as well as religious significance. The main feature in the nave is the large iconostasis. Also of interest are the large copper font (1685) and the cases in front of the iconostasis containing Gospel books, liturgical utensils, etc.

Church of the Dormition

The Smolensk Cathedral was the nuns' summer church, with no form of heating. In winter they used the Cathedral of the Dormition, which was heated. This church and the adjoining Refectory were built by Regent Sofya Alekseevna in the 1780s.

Obelisk of Great Revolutionaries and Thinkers

See Alexander Garden

Polytechnic Museum (Politeknichesky Muzey) K13 (E1)

Location
3–4 New Square
(Novaya Ploshchad 3–4)

Metro
Dzerzhinskaya

The Polytechnic Museum illustrates the technological development of the Soviet State with some 20,000 exhibits displayed in just under sixty rooms. The exhibits are arranged and explained in exemplary fashion, with dioramas, experiments, machines, models and even robots speaking several

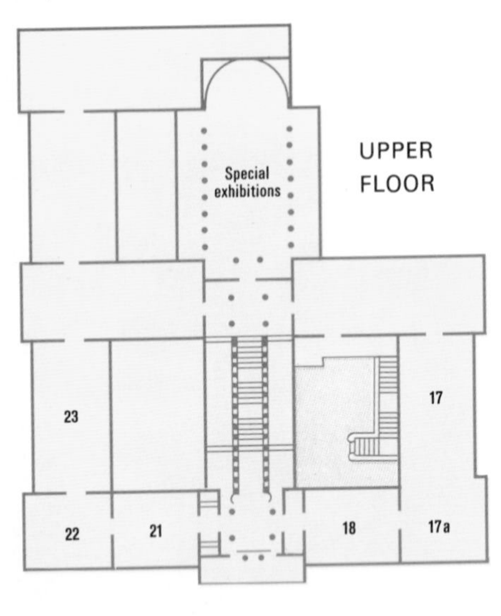

UPPER FLOOR (numbered rooms)
19th and 20th c. European art
- 17 Bonnard, Denis, Derain, Vlaminck, Fries, Marquet, Redon, Rouault, H. Rousseau, Signac, Utrillo, Van Dongen, Vuillard
- 17a Matisse, Picasso
- 18 Cézanne, Gauguin, Van Gogh
- 21 Degas, Manet, Monet, Pissarro, Renoir, Sisley
- 22 Bastien-Lepage, Böcklin, Bonnat, Carrière, Cassatt, Feuerbach, Forain, Fortuny, Liebermann, Loir, Menzel, Meunier, Munch, Munkáczy, Puvis de Chavannes, Raffaelli, Whistler, Zorn, Zuluaga
- 23 Boudin, Constable, Corot, Courbet, David, Delacroix, Diaz de la Peña, Dupré, Gérard, Géricault, Gros, Guérin, Lawrence, Millet, Opie, T. Rousseau, Troyon, Vernet

UPPER FLOOR (unnumbered rooms)
Egyptian art (Golenishchev Collection)
Ancient art
Originals and casts of sculpture; Greek vases; antiquities from the Black Sea region
German painting (partly in store)
Friedrich, Hodler, Kauffmann, Lenbach, Liss, Makart, Mengs

Muzey Izobrazitelnykh Iskusstv imeni Pushkina

Pushkin Museum of Fine Art

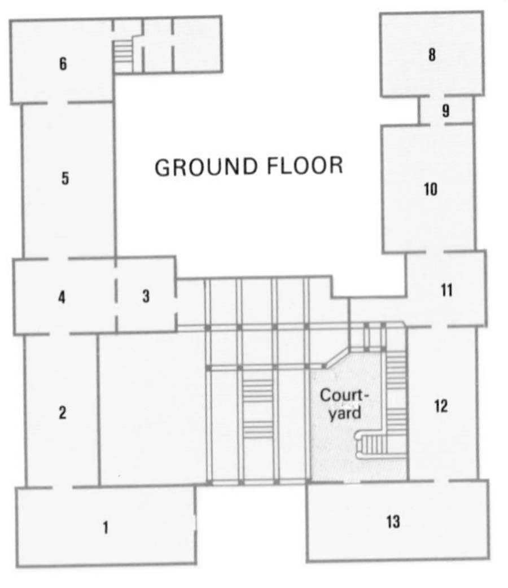

GROUND FLOOR
- 1,2 Ancient Orient
  Material from Urartu and Nisa
- 3 Coptic and Byzantine art
- 4 13th–15th c. Italian painting
- 5 15th–16th c. Italian painting
  Botticelli, Bordone, Bronzino, Crivelli, Salviati, Tintoretto, Veronese
- 6 15th–16th c. German and Netherlands painting
  Beukelaer, Cranach, Master of Messkirch
- 8 17th c. Flemish painting
  Bruegel, Jordaens, Rubens, Van Dyck
- 9 16th–17th c. Netherlands painting
- 10 17th c. Dutch painting
  Metsu, Rembrandt, Terborch, Van Ruisdael
- 11 Spanish, Italian and German Baroque painting
  El Greco, Guercini, Murillo, Zurbarán
- 12 17th–18th c. Italian painting
  Bellotto, Canaletto, Guardi, Tiepolo
- 13 17th–18th c. French painting
  Boucher, Drouais, Fragonard, Greuze, Lorrain, Poussin, Watteau
- Court-yard (modelled on courtyard of the Bargello in Florence)
  Casts of originals of the medieval period (Golden Door of Freiberg Cathedral, Saxony) and Renaissance (Michelangelo, Verrocchio)

Pushkin Museum of Fine Art

languages, all helping to demonstrate and make comprehensible the complicated processes of nuclear technology, telecommunications and television, mining, computers, automobile manufacture, etc. The museum is housed in an imposing building erected in the second half of the 19th c. in a pastiche of Old Russian style.

**Pushkin Museum of Fine Art

(Muzey Izobrazitelnykh Iskusstv imeni Pushkina)

H11

In spite of its name the Pushkin Museum of Fine Art has nothing to do with the great Russian poet (Pushkin House: see Practical Information – Museums). The nucleus of the museum was a collection of casts of Classical sculpture established in 1912. Its resources were dramatically increased, however, after the October Revolution, when large private collections were taken over by the State and it also acquired many works of art from museums in Leningrad.

The Pushkin Museum now possesses a large collection of antiquities from the Near East, Egypt, Greece and Byzantium, as well as numerous casts of Antique and Renaissance works of sculpture. It owes its international reputation, however, to its extensive holdings of European (non-Russian) painting. Its main strength lies in the French schools, from the Neo-classical artists (David, Fragonard, Watteau, Poussin) by way of the Impressionists (Cézanne, Manet, Monet, Gauguin) to the beginnings of modern art (Matisse). Italian painters (Botticelli, Perugino, Tiepolo), Flemish (Rubens, Jordaens, Van Dyck), Dutch

Location
12 Volkhonka Street
(Volkhonka Ulitsa 12)

Metro
Kropotkinskaya

Opening times
Wed.–Mon. 10 a.m.–8 p.m.

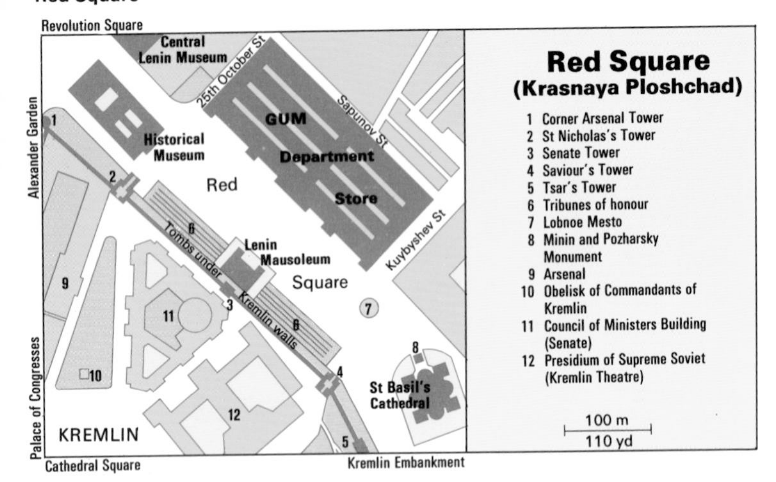

(Rembrandt, de Hooch) and Spanish painters (El Greco, Murillo, Velázquez, Zurbarán, Picasso) are also well represented.

Special exhibitions

The Pushkin Museum frequently puts on special exhibitions: for information about these, apply to Intourist (see Practical Information – Information).

** Red Square (Krasnaya Ploshchad) J12 (D1)

Metro
Ploshchad Revolutsii

Red Square, with an average length of 400 m (440 yd) and an average breadth of 150 m (165 yd), is the central square not only of Moscow but of the whole Soviet Union. Since the time of Ivan III (15th c.) this has been the scene of great public events, mainly political – rallies, demonstrations, processions. In earlier times Red Square was also a place of execution. Its name does not, however, come from the blood which has been spilt here: in Old Slavonic *krasny*, "red", also meant "beautiful", since red was regarded as a particularly beautiful colour. The translation "Red Square" instead of "Beautiful Square" which is now universally used, became established only in the 20th c.

Every year on 7 November a military parade is held in Red Square to mark the anniversary of the October Revolution (on the date, see Practical Information – Calendar). On that day, too, and on 1 May (Labour Day) there are parades of the workers of the Soviet Union which have something of the air of a popular festival.

Before the October Revolution official proclamations were read out in Red Square, and it was also the scene of markets, fairs and religious festivals, including the Palm Sunday procession when the Patriarch, mounted on an ass, and the Tsar with their retinues made their way into the Kremlin through the Saviour's Gate-Tower. Here, too, public executions were carried out; from here Russian forces led by Minin and Pozharsky launched

Red Square from St Basil's Cathedral

the attack which recovered the Kremlin from the Poles in 1612; and here after the Second World War the flags of the German Wehrmacht were brought in triumph and burned in front of the Lenin Mausoleum.

Originally the approach to the Kremlin from Red Square was protected by a moat, 32 m (105 ft) wide and 12 m (40 ft) deep, between the Neglinnaya and the Moskva. During the reconstruction and rebuilding carried out under the direction of Osip I. Bove to make good the damage caused by the French in 1812 the moat was filled in, the Neglinnaya was bricked over and the drawbridges in front of the Saviour's Tower and St Nicholas's Tower were removed.

Red Square is bounded on the south-west by the walls of the Kremlin with their numerous towers and two gate-towers. At the north end is the picturesque building occupied by the Historical Museum, with the Central Lenin Museum (see entry) to its right, in Revolution Square. Most of the north-east side of Red Square is occupied by the GUM Department Store, facing the Lenin Mausoleum and the tombs of prominent Soviet citizens below the Kremlin walls. At the south end of the square is St Basil's Cathedral.

*Lenin Mausoleum (Mavzoley Lenina)

Opening times
Summer: Tues.–Thurs. and Sat. 9 a.m.–1 p.m., Sun. 9 a.m.–2 p.m.
Winter: Tues.–Thurs. and Sat. 11 a.m.–2 p.m., Sun. 11 a.m.–4 p.m.

Even visitors who are against Lenin or indifferent to him will find it worth while, for the sake of the experience, to join the queue – sometimes apparently endless, particularly in summer – and go down into the air-conditioned vault in which the embalmed body of the founder of the Soviet State lies in a glass coffin.

The Lenin Mausoleum occupies the site of the temporary

Sentries on guard at the Lenin Mausoleum

Changing of the guard

wooden mausoleum in which Lenin's body was deposited on 27 January 1924 after the official funeral ceremony. The Lenin Funeral Train Museum (see Practical Information – Museums) contains models of this temporary structure and photographic material covering the days between Lenin's death and burial.
The present mausoleum, on the highest point in Red Square, in front of the Senate Tower of the Kremlin (see entry), was built in 1930 to the design of Aleksey V. Shchusev. On either side are the Tribunes of honour, with seating for 10,000 spectators. The Mausoleum – which also serves as a reviewing platform for members of the Government – is built of dark red granite in a series of receding tiers, with a mourning band of black labradorite encircling the whole structure.

Interior

From the entrance, which is surmounted by the name "Lenin" in inlaid porphyry letters and flanked by two sentries, twenty-three porphyry steps lead down into the semi-darkness of the air-conditioned burial vault, which is faced with black and grey labradorite, with porphyry pilasters. Lenin's body, embalmed by a special process, lies in a glass coffin. Visitors are allowed only a few moments to look at the body as they walk round it: they are not permitted to pause and hold up the queue.
In the absolute silence that prevails in the vault, undisturbed by the clicking of cameras, even Western visitors may be impressed by this glimpse of the mortal remains of a man who was one of the great world figures of this century and is still the idol and spiritual father of millions in both East and West. The mausoleum seems designed to produce a kind of quasi-religious awe – even though this runs counter to the views of Lenin himself, who throughout his life rejected any kind of personality cult.
Photography is prohibited in the burial vault, and cameras, if carried, should be kept closed. Foreigners can join the queue, which is often hundreds of yards long, outside the cloakroom of the Historical Museum, where large cases, cameras, etc., should be left.

Changing of the guard

The guard at the entrance to the mausoleum is changed every hour on the hour. Exactly 2 minutes and 45 seconds before the hour the two relieving sentries emerge from the Saviour's Gate-Tower and march to the entrance of the mausoleum, taking up their position as the clock strikes in the tower.

Tombs below the Kremlin walls

Behind the Lenin Mausoleum, separated from Red Square by a row of silver firs, the remains of the Soviet Union's honoured dead are buried – revolutionaries and politicians, cosmonauts and foreign Communist leaders, Lenin's sister, and the symbolic 500 revolutionaries killed in the October Revolution. Many of the names recorded here in tablets set into the Kremlin walls will be encountered by visitors as they go about Moscow, in the names of streets, buildings, parks, societies, etc.
It is mostly politicians who are buried here, the most recent addition being Suslov (d. 1982), the great ideologist of the Party. Others include Mikhail I. Kalinin (see Kalinin Avenue); Lenin's wife Nadezhda K. Krupskaya; Stalin, who was originally buried in the Mausoleum beside Lenin; the German Communist Clara Zetkin; Arthur MacManus, one of the

Memorials of the honoured dead, Kremlin walls

founders of the British Communist Party; William D. Haywood of Chicago; and such leading Soviet figures as S. M. Kirov, V. V. Kuibyshev, A. V. Lunacharsky and G. K. Ordzhonikidze. Among cosmonauts buried here are Yury A. Gagarin, the first man (in 1961) to circle the earth in a space capsule, who was killed in a flying accident in 1968, and the three cosmonauts who died during the re-entry of their space craft in 1971.

*Historical Museum (Istorichesky Muzey)

Location
1–2 Red Square
(Krasnaya Ploshchad 1–2)

Metro
Ploshchad Revolutsii

Opening times
Mon. and Thurs.–Sat.
10.30 a.m.–5.30 p.m., Wed. and Sun. noon–7 p.m.

Closed
Tues. and last day of month

The Historical Museum, first opened in 1883, is the largest and most important museum devoted to the history of the peoples of the Soviet Union from prehistoric times to the present day. Its 44,000 exhibits, in forty-eight rooms, illustrate and document the history of Russia and the Soviet Union from the Palaeolithic period, Kievan Russia, the dominance of the Golden Horde and the beginnings of the principality of Moscow to the consolidation of the centralised State, the cultural history of Russia in the 17th–19th c. and the Communist movement centred on Lenin.
Following the foundation of the Historical Museum in 1872, work began in 1874 on the construction of the present building, designed by Aleksandr A. Semyonov and Vladimir O. Sherwood, with its façade in the Old Russian style. The architects were concerned to fit the building into the architectural pattern of Red Square, taking as their models St Basil's Cathedral and the Kremlin walls.
The interior was designed by Aleksandr P. Popov, and the museum was opened to the public in 1883. The holdings of the

Façade of the Historical Museum, in Old Russian style ▶

museum have swollen – by gifts and donations, but mainly by the acquisition of material from all over the Soviet Union following the nationalisation of land and property – to such an extent that it cannot display even a tenth of what it possesses.

Branches of the Museum

St Basil's Cathedral, the 16th and 17th c. mansions in Razin Street, the museum in the Novodevichy Convent (see entry) and the Kolomenskoe Museum (see Practical Information – Excursions) are all branches of the Historical Museum.

*GUM Department Store

Location
3 Red Square
(Krasnaya Ploshchad 3)

Opening Times
Mon.–Sat. 8 a.m.–9 p.m.

Opposite the Lenin Mausoleum, on the north-east side of Red Square, is the Soviet Union's largest department store, the Gosudarstvenny Universalny Magazin (State Universal Store), or GUM for short. This huge complex, 252 m (825 ft) long by 90 m (295 ft) across, was built between 1888 and 1894, replacing the old "Trading Rows" which had previously occupied the site. Restored in the 1950s, its three storeys now house 150 separate shops which attract some 400,000 customers every day.

GUM is very different from a Western department store: a more appropriate comparison would be with a Western shopping centre. But instead of American-style glass and concrete architecture GUM has ornate bridges and gangways, Old Russian shop-fronts, chandeliers, mirror walls and much stucco ornament.

Inside GUM

Lobnoe Mesto: place of execution in Tsarist times

A general view of the interior can be had from the balustrade above the fountain in the centre of the complex. The swarming crowds of shoppers, in all the nationalities of the Soviet Union, make a spectacle which will be one of the visitor's memories of Moscow.

On the ground floor are a number of shops selling souvenirs.

Lobnoe Mesto (Place of Skulls)

The Lobnoe Mesto (Place of Skulls) is a circular stone platform near the south end of Red Square, approached by a short flight of steps and closed by wrought-iron gates, from which the decrees of the Tsars and Patriarchs were read out. It was also a place of execution, although most executions were carried out not on the stone platform itself but on temporary wooden scaffolds erected in front of it.

In 1606 the corpse of the False Dmitry was burned here and the ashes fired from a cannon towards the west, the direction from which the hated Polish Catholics had come. In 1671 Stenka Razin, leader of the first large peasant rising, was executed and dismembered here. Here, too, 2000 rebellious Streltsy were executed in 1698, when Peter the Great is said to have struck off the first ten heads with his own hand. (The scene is depicted in Surikov's painting, "The Morning of the Execution of the Streltsy in Red Square", now in the Tretyakov Gallery: see p. 123.) The public execution of the great Cossack rebel Pugachov also took place here in 1775.

Monument to Minin and Pozharsky

The Monument to Minin and Pozharsky, in front of St Basil's Cathedral, was Moscow's first patriotic monument, unveiled in 1818. It was the work of the Neo-classical sculptor Ivan Petrovich Martos, who spent almost fourteen years, with interruptions, on the task. The cost was met by public subscription.

The monument was moved to its present position after the construction of the Lenin Mausoleum. Note the position of Minin's right arm, pointing towards the Kremlin.

Kuzma Minich Minin (d. 1616) was a butcher of Nizhny Novgorod (known since 1932 as Gorky) who in 1611 formed a popular militia to fight the invading Poles and persuaded Prince Dmitry Mikhailovich Pozharsky (1578–1642) to become its commander.

Pozharsky's forces soon swelled into a considerable army. In the spring of 1612 he moved to Yaroslavl, and on 26 March set out for Moscow. A Polish army was routed in August, and on 22 October Pozharsky took Kitay-Gorod (the trading district off Red Square). Soon afterwards the Kremlin was captured, and on 27 October 1612 the Poles surrendered.

On the granite base of the monument are bronze reliefs of "Citizens of Nizhny Novgorod" and "The Surrender of the Poles". The figures of Minin and Pozharsky are also cast in bronze – Minin pointing towards the goal of the patriotic forces, the Kremlin, and Pozharsky still hesitating to take command.

** St Basil's Cathedral (Pokrovsky Sobor Vasiliya Blazhennogo)

Opening times
Wed.–Sun. 9.30 a.m.–5 p.m.,
Mon. 10.30 a.m.–2.30 p.m.

Many would think that St Basil's Cathedral alone would justify a visit to Moscow. This extraordinary building – the supreme achievement of 16th c. architecture in Moscow – is now a branch of the Historical Museum. Until 1978 the cathedral, with its ground-plan in the form of an eight-pointed star, its nine churches and its bizarre domes, its vivid colours and its heterogeneous assortment of architectural elements, could be seen only from the outside; but the interior has recently been excellently restored and is now open to the public.

History

The church was originally built by Ivan the Terrible in 1555–61 as the Cathedral of the Intercession of the Virgin (Pokrovsky Sobor) to commemorate the capture of Kazan, capital of the khanate of Kazan, on the festival of the Intercession of the Virgin in 1552.

According to the chronicler the architects of the cathedral, Postnik and Barma, were sent to Ivan the Terrible by God. The story that the Tsar had them blinded after the building was completed, however, is no more than a legend, for in 1588, four years after Ivan's death, Postnik and Barma added the chapel at the north-east corner of the cathedral housing the tomb of the holy fool Basil (Vasily) by whose name the cathedral is now known.

The holy fools, or fools in Christ, were itinerant ascetics who enjoyed great popularity among the ordinary people of Russia, many of them being revered as saints.

The holy fool Basil the Blessed died in 1552, the year of the capture of Kazan. He was well known for his fearless

St Basil's Cathedral ▶

denunciation of Ivan the Terrible's cruelties; and when, after Ivan's death, his chapel was built on to the cathedral the name of the chapel gradually came to be applied to the whole cathedral.
The domes were given their present form at the end of the 16th c. To refer to them as onion domes seems an over-simplification, given their varied turban-like and tear-drop shapes. Originally the domes were helm-shaped, with eight domes set round the central tower (destroyed at the end of the 18th c.). The colourful painting of the domes dates from the 17th c., when the bell-tower was added and the open galleries round the whole complex were vaulted over.
In 1812 the French stabled their horses in St Basil's Cathedral. Before leaving Moscow Napoleon ordered it to be blown up; but cold, hunger and fear of sabotage by the people of Moscow prevented the order from being carried out.

Ground-plan and exterior

Although St Basil's Cathedral looks such a confusion of chapels, galleries, loggias and domes it is actually based on strictly geometrical principles. In the centre is the principal church with its 57 m (187 ft) high tower, its octagonal tent roof topped by a small dome, rising high above the other structures. Round this central tower are four large and four small chapels, with domes proportional to their size. The four larger chapels are at the ends of an imaginary cross with the principal church at its central point; the smaller chapels lie between the larger ones.
These nine churches stand on a high brick-built base with arcading and pillars. The four larger chapels have an octagonal lower storey topped by a series of triangles enclosing slit windows; the apexes of the triangles point upwards, giving the tower a strong sense of vertical movement. Above these are a cornice and a band of blind semicircular arches, and above these again are more triangles and slit windows, maintaining the upward movement.
The towers of the four smaller chapels begin with tiers of blind

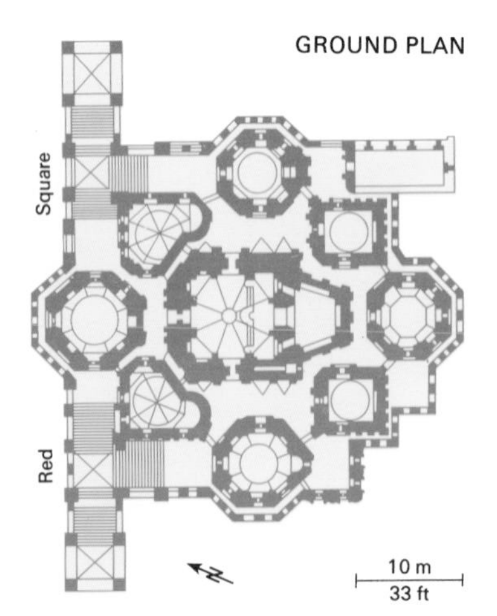

St Basil's Cathedral Pokrovsky Sobor Vasiliya Blazhennogo

St Basil's Cathedral, properly the Cathedral of the Intercession of the Virgin, is described in Baedeker's "Russia" (first English edition, 1914) as follows:

". . . It consists of eleven small dark chapels, arranged in two storeys, and combined in a most extraordinary agglomeration. The building is surmounted by a dozen domes and spires, painted in all the colours of the rainbow and of the most varied forms. Some of them are shaped like bulbs or pineapples, some are twisted in strange spirals, some are serrated, some covered with facets or scales. All of them bulge out over their supporting drums and are crowned by massive crosses. The decoration, in which numerous Renaissance details may be detected, is of the most exuberant character. The whole effect is quaint and fantastic in the extreme."

Interior of St Basil's Cathedral

semicircular arches, set back above one another. Above these is the drum supporting the dome, with brick mosaic decoration and slit windows.

Interior

Since St Basil's Cathedral was conceived as a monument commemorating the capture of Kazan, the interior is less impressive than the grandiose exterior. It is still, however, worth seeing.
Its most notable features are the frescoes in the central tower and the passages and galleries, mostly of the 16th c. The icons date from the 15th–17th c.

Exhibition

In two rooms under the bell-tower is a exhibition on the theme "The Pokrovsky Cathedral as an Example of 16th Century Architecture", with old prints, sketches, plans and drawings illustrating the history of the cathedral.

Kremlin towers in Red Square

The most northerly tower on this side of the Kremlin, the Corner Arsenal tower, is best seen from the Alexander Garden (see entry).

St Nicholas's Tower

The 70 m (230 ft) high St Nicholas's Gate-Tower was built in 1491 by Pietro Antonio Solari. From this gate a road once led to a monastery (destroyed) dedicated to St Nicholas, and there was a mosaic icon of the Saint on the gateway.

In 1812 the tower was blown up by the French and badly damaged. It was restored in 1816 under the direction of Osip I. Bove, who also filled in the moat between the Kremlin and Red Square and removed the drawbridge which spanned the moat outside St Nicholas's Tower.
At the same time Luigi Rusca built the 15 m (50 ft) high neo-Gothic superstructure, modelled on the 13th–15th c. St Mary's Church in Stargard (Pomerania; now in Poland).
Like most of the Kremlin towers, St Nicholas's Tower is crowned by a five-pointed Soviet star.

Senate Tower

Immediately behind the Lenin Mausoleum is the Senate Tower, also built in 1491 by Pietro Antonio Solari. It was given its present name after the building of the Senate (1776–87; now Council of Ministers Building, Kremlin – see entry), just inside the walls at this point.
The superstructure dates from 1680.

*Saviour's Tower (Spasskaya Bashnya)

No admission

The 70 m (230 ft) high Saviour's Tower is the most magnificent of the Kremlin towers, the very symbol and emblem of Moscow. From time immemorial it has been the principal entrance to the Kremlin.
The tower, like its two neighbours to the north, was built in 1491 by Pietro Antonio Solari. The tent-roofed superstructure was added in 1624–25 by Christopher Galloway or Halloway and Bazhen Ogurtsov, and a clock and carillon were installed by Galloway. The present clock, by the Butenop brothers, dates from 1852; the gigantic mechanism of the carillon occupies three storeys of the tower.
Until the October Revolution the carillon played the Tsarist National Anthem, and between 1917 and 1941 it played the "Internationale". The clock now only strikes the hours; it is broadcast on Soviet radio at 6 a.m., 12 noon and midnight.
The tower was given its name in 1658, when an icon of Christ was set up over the entrance. Before the October Revolution men were required to take their hats off when passing through the gate.

Tsar's Tower/Tsar's Pavilion

The Tsar's Tower or Tsar's Pavilion, near the Saviour's Tower, was built only in 1680, when the other towers were given their present superstructures.
It is said that Ivan the Terrible used to sit in a wooden pavilion here to watch executions in Red Square: hence the name of the tower.

Alarm Tower (Nabatnaya Bashnya)

The name of this tower indicates its function: in case of impending danger the alarm bell (*nabat*) was rung here.

Superstructure of Saviour's Tower

Tsar's Tower

During a rising in 1771 the rebels rang the alarm bell: whereupon Catherine the Great, after crushing the revolt with troops from St Petersburg, had the clapper of the bell removed. Since 1821 the bell has been kept in the Armoury in the Kremlin (see entry).

Constantine and Helena Gate-Tower

The Constantine and Helena Gate-Tower takes its name from a monastery in the Kremlin, now destroyed, which was dedicated to the Emperor Constantine and his mother Helena (both saints of the Orthodox Church).
The tower was built in 1490 by Pietro Antonio Solari. The superstructure, like those of other Kremlin towers, was added in 1680.

Beklemishev Tower

The Beklemishev Tower, which is just under 47 m (155 ft) high, was built by Marco Ruffo (Mark Fryazin) in 1487. The superstructure dates from the 1680s.
The tower is named after a boyar called Beklemishev who had a mansion just inside the Kremlin walls at this point. After Beklemishev was executed in the reign of Ivan III the tower was used as a prison.
The tower's tent roof was partly demolished during the October Revolution but was restored to its original state in the 1950s.

Beklemishev Tower; in background the Ukraina Hotel

Rublyov Museum of Old Russian Art

See Andronikov Monastery

St Basil's Cathedral

See Red Square

Saviour's Tower

See Red Square

Schusev Museum of Architecture

H12

(Muzey Arkhitektury imeni Shchuseva)

Location
5 Kalinin Avenue
(Prospekt Kalinina 5)

Metro
Biblioteka im. Lenina,
Arbatskaya

The Shchusev Museum gives an excellent survey of Russian architecture from Kievan Russia (St Sophia Cathedral, Kiev) to the tower blocks of the present day with the help of models, sketches, photographs, plans, etc.
The museum is named after the great Soviet architect Aleksey Viktorovich Shchusev (1873–1949), who designed, among much else, the Kazan Station and the Lenin Mausoleum in Red

Square (see entry), which show Shchusev's development from the Old Russian or "fairy-tale" style to a restrained and sober monumental style. Shchusev also played an important part in the urban planning of modern Moscow.
There is a branch of the Shchusev Museum in the Don Monastery (see entry).

*Television Tower (Televizionnaya Bashnya) H17

The Television Tower, to the north of Moscow, is the second highest tower of its kind (537 m (1762 ft)). Pencil-slim for most of its height, it swells at the foot into a conical base which rests on ten concrete supports. Fast lifts take visitors up to the various viewing platforms and the revolving restaurant at 330 m (985 ft). It is advisable to book tables in the restaurant through Intourist (see Practical Information – Information).
In a wind of any strength the tower sways quite perceptibly: the timid have been warned!

Location
Murmansk Passage
(Murmansky Proezd)

Metro
VDNKh

Railway station
Ostankino

Tomb of the Unknown Soldier

See Alexander Garden

**Tretyakov Gallery (Tretyakovskaya Galereya) J10

The Tretyakov Gallery is the world's greatest gallery of Russian painting and sculpture from the 11th c. to the present day. Its particular strengths lie in its medieval Russian icons and modern Russian art (late 19th c. Realism, the Socialist Realism of the Soviet period). With a total of some 50,000 works of painting, graphic art, sculpture and applied art the Tretyakov is also one of the largest museums in the world.
It is advisable to obtain tickets in advance through Intourist (see Practical Information – Information). Without such a ticket there may be a long wait for admission, since the Tretyakov attracts some 4000 visitors every day.

Location
10 Lavrushin Lane
(Lavrushinsky Pereulok 10)

Metro
Novokuznetskaya

Opening times
Tues.–Sun. 10 a.m.–8 p.m.

Closed
Mon. and first day of month

History

The founder of the gallery was the Moscow businessman, collector and art patron Pavel Mikhailovich Tretyakov (1832–98), who presented to the city of Moscow in 1892 the collection of Russian art which he and his brother Sergey had systematically built up from 1856 onwards. There is a portrait of Pavel Tretyakov (by Ivan N. Kramskoy, 1876) in Room 14.
The gallery's present main building was erected in 1901–02, near the Tretyakov mansion, to the design of the "fairy-tale" painter Viktor M. Vasnetsov (see Vasnetsov House). Vasnetsov was one of the group of artists who gathered under the aegis of the industrialist and art patron Savva I. Mamontov on his estate of Abramtsevo near Zagorsk (see Practical Information – Excursions) and were largely instrumental in promoting the return to old Slav traditions which reached its full flowering in Russian Realism and Art Nouveau. The building is in the Old Russian or "fairy-tale" style characteristic of the turn of the century, the Russian version of Art Nouveau.

Façade of the Tretyakov Gallery

The gallery, originally known as the O. and I. Tretyakov Municipal Art Gallery, was taken into State ownership by a decree of the Soviet Government on 3 July 1918.
The collection, enormously increased by the nationalisation of private property, the incorporation of private collections and new acquisitions, soon outgrew the capacity of the original building, and a new right wing was added by Aleksey V. Shchusev in 1927–35.
Since then the shortage of space has become still more acute. The store-rooms of the Tretyakov Gallery are full of works by modern Russian painters (Chagall, Kandinsky, Falk, Malevich, etc.) which can not be exhibited for lack of space; and the same problem also affects the gallery's icons. A new Tretyakov Gallery has been under construction for some years on the banks of the Moskva opposite the Gorky Park of Culture and Recreation, and when completed this will house the collection of modern Russian and Soviet art.
A tour of the Tretyakov Gallery – which it is estimated would involve a walk of 80 km (50 miles), going from picture to picture, for a determined visitor who wanted to see everything – makes quite a demand on the stamina of even a selective visitor (though he may be able to have an occasional rest on one of the wooden chairs provided).
One consequence of the lack of space is that the pictures tend to be hung very close together and sometimes in curious juxtaposition, with insignificant pictures alongside important ones, though often in splendid frames.
The following notes pick out the most important artists and works.

Tretyakovskaya Galereya — Tretyakov Gallery

UPPER FLOOR

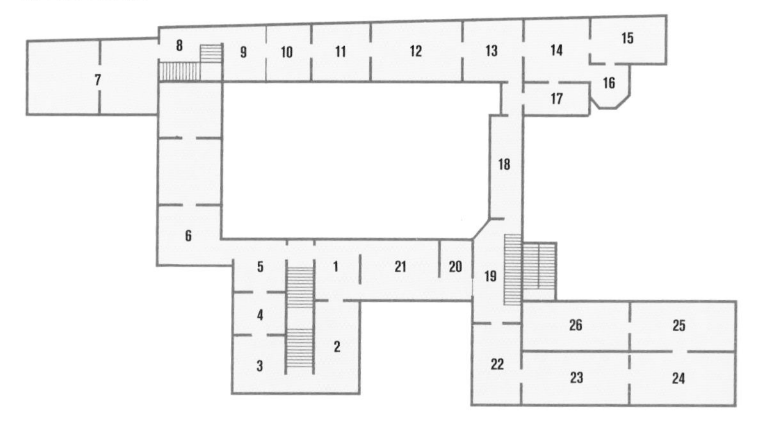

The nucleus of the **Tretyakov Gallery** was a private collection formed by the Moscow businessman Pavel Mikhailovich Tretyakov (1832–98) and his brother Sergey. In 1918 it became a national museum of Russian painting and sculpture. The present building, in the Old Russian style, was erected in 1901–02 to the design of the painter Viktor Mikhailovich Vasnetsov and enlarged in 1927–35; but even the enlarged gallery can show only a fraction of its total holdings. A new gallery is under construction a short distance away to the south-west, on the banks of the Moskva.

GROUND FLOOR

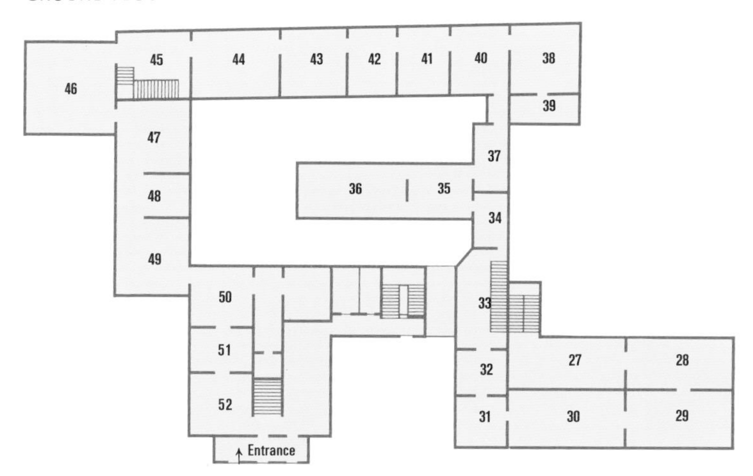

1700–1850

Room 5:
Vladimir Lukich Borovikovsky (1757–1825): portraits of the St Petersburg aristocracy.
Dmitry Grigorevich Levitsky (*c.* 1735–1822): portraits of the St Petersburg aristocracy; "P. A. Demidov in the Garden of his Mansion" (1733).

Room 6:
D. G. Levitsky: more portraits.
Fyodor Yakovlevich Alekseev (*c.* 1754–1824), the first Russian painter of *vedute*, known as the "Russian Canaletto" (trained at the St Petersburg Academy and in Italy): "View of the Palace Embankment from the Peter and Paul Fortress" (1794); views of the Kremlin, Moscow, *c.* 1810–20.
Orest Adamovich Kiprensky (1782–1836; portraits under the influence of Van Dyck; in Italy from 1816): "Darya Nikolaevna Khvostova" (1814), "Self-Portrait" (1822–23), "Aleksandr Pushkin" (1827).
Silvestr Feodosievich Shchedrin (1791–1830; painter of landscapes and *vedute*; in Italy from 1818): "On the Tiber in Rome" (1824), "Walk on the Terrace" (1828).

Room 7:
Karl Pavlovich Bryullov (1799–1852; studied in Italy, then professor at St Petersburg Academy; historical painter, one of the leading representatives of the Romantic school): "Self-Portrait" (1848).
Aleksandr Andreevich Ivanov (1806–58; long stay in Rome from 1830 onwards; religious themes in tradition of Antiquity, the Renaissance and the German Nazarenes; a forerunner of Russian Realism): "Christ shows himself to the People" (1837–57, with some 700 sketches and preliminary studies), "Pontine Marshes" (1838), "Via Appia at Sunset" (1845).

Room 9:
Alekseey Gavrilovich Venetsianov (1780–1847; realistic portraits and landscapes, genre scenes): "Peasant Girl at her Embroidery" (1843).
Pavel Andreevich Fedotov (1815–52; satirist and social critic, influenced by 17th c. Dutch genre painting): "The Penniless Major's Wooing" (1848).

Peredvizhniki (Itinerants)

The Tretyakov Gallery has an excellent representation of works by the Peredvizhniki or Itinerants, a group of artists founded by Ivan N. Kramskoy in 1870 under the name "Society for Travelling Exhibitions". The members of the group had either been excluded from the St Petersburg Academy or had distanced themselves from it, since they were opposed to the pro-Western views of the artistic establishment and called for a return to Slav themes. The society began with a number of highly successful exhibitions in St Petersburg, Moscow, Kiev and Kharkov, and then sought to appeal to a wider public, mainly middle class, with some fifty travelling exhibitions a year. They received valuable support from Pavel Tretyakov, who bought their works and thus provided the nucleus of the gallery's present collection.
The group went in for what was called Critical Realism, not only in psychologically searching portraits but also in landscapes, historical pictures and genre scenes. They would have nothing to do with "art for art's sake". Since the Itinerants also painted

In the Tretyakov Gallery

pictures of social criticism they are now highly rated as forerunners of Socialist Realism. They group broke up in 1923. The following rooms are almost exclusively devoted to the Itinerants.

1850–1900

Rooms 10 and 12:
Ivan Konstantinovich Aivazovsky (1817–1900; seascapes and landscapes in the manner of the Russian Late Romantic school, also naval battles).

Room 11:
Vasily Grigoryevich Perov (1834–82; studied in Paris, came under influence of Courbet; founding-member of the Itinerants group; realistic portraits of the Russian intelligentsia; genre scenes of popular life, with strong social criticism and satirical depiction of the clergy; painting style predominantly Neo-classical): "Easter Procession" (1861), "Funeral" (1865), "Troika – Three Children with Sledges" (1866), "Aleksandr Ostrovsky" (1871), "Dostoevsky" (1872), "In the Monastery Refectory", etc.

Room 13:
Konstantin Apollonovich Savitsky (1844–1905; a member of the Itinerants group; mainly mass scenes): "Repair Work on the Railway" (1874), "Receiving the Icon" (1878).
Korsukhin (1835–94); Vasily Maksimov (1844–1911).

Room 14:
Ivan Nikolaevich Kramskoy (1837–87; principal founder and leader of the Itinerants; great influence of Ilya Repin; mainly

psychological portraits and genre scenes): "Christ in the Wilderness" (1872; taken as a symbol of the progressive Russian intelligentsia), "Tolstoy" (1873), "Pavel Tretyakov" (1876), "Nikolay Nekrasov" (1877), "Peasant Girl with Blue Head-Scarf" (1882), "Portrait of an Unknown Woman" (1884), "Inconsolable Grief" (1884).

Room 15:
Nikolay Nikolaevich Gay (1831–94; founding-member of Itinerants group; portraits, Biblical and historical pictures; dramatic chiaroscuro effects): "Tolstoy" (1884), "What is Truth?" (1890), "Golgotha" (1892, unfinished).

Room 16:
Fyodor Aleksandrovich Vasilyev (1850–73; landscapes; influence on Ilya Repin).
Aleksey Kondratyevich Savrasov (1830–97; founding-member of Itinerants group; landscapes): "Crows after the Grain" (1871).

Room 17:
Vladimir Egorovich Makovsky (1846–1920; member of Itinerants group from 1872; genre scenes, with strong social criticism, almost caricatural; illustrations to Gogol): "In the Doctor's Waiting-Room" (1870), "Bank Failure" (1881).

Room 18:
Nikolay Aleksandrovich Yaroshenko (1846–98; member of Itinerants group; portraits, landscapes, social criticism; drawings): "Stoker" (1878).

Room 19:
Ivan Ivanovich Shishkin (1832–98; after training in Moscow and St Petersburg travelled to Germany and Switzerland; founding-member of Itinerants group; from 1872 at St Petersburg Academy): "Midday near Moscow" (1869).

Room 21:
Isaak Ilyich Levitan: see Room 29.

Room 22:
Viktor Mikhailovich Vasnetsov (1848–1926; member of Itinerants group from 1874; historical painting with fantastic elements; scenes from fairy-tales and legends; frescoes, stage sets; two museums in Moscow devoted to his work, see Practical Information – Museums): "Apartments of Count Berendey" (1885; stage set for Rimsky-Korsakov's "Snow Maiden").

Room 23:
Vasily Vasilyevich Vereshchagin (1842–1904; landscapes, Oriental scenes, anti-war pictures): "Apotheosis of War" or "Hill or Skulls" (1871), "Riders in Jaipur" (1882–83).

Room 24:
Vasily Ivanovich Surikov (1848–1916; member of Itinerants group from 1882; realistic historical paintings): "The Morning of the Execution of the Streltsy in Red Square" (1878–81), "Aleksandr D. Menshikov at Beresov", "Departure of Boyarynya Morozova" (1887).

Vasily Surikov's "Morning of the Execution of the Streltsy" (1881)

Rooms 25 and 26:
Ilya Efimovich Repin (1844–1930; the great master of Russian Realism, who prepared the way for the Itinerants): "Volga Boatmen" (1872), "Religious Procession" (1880–83), "Arrest of a Political Agitator in a Village" (1878), "Unexpected Return of a Political Exile" (1884), "Ivan the Terrible with his Fatally Injured Son" (1885), "The Composer Modest Mussorgsky" (1881), "Tolstoy" (1887), "Tolstoy resting in the Forest" (1891), "The Zaporozhian Cossacks writing a Letter to the Turkish Sultan" (1891).

Room 28:
Vasily Dmitrievich Polenov (1844–1927; member of Itinerants group from 1878; teacher at Moscow School of Art 1882–95; genre scenes, historical pictures, portraits): "Moscow Courtyard", "Grandmother's Garden" (both 1878).

Room 29:
Isaak Ilyich Levitan (1860–1900; one of the leading Russian landscape-painters of the 19th c., influenced by the French Impressionists): "After the Rain" (1889), "The Evening Bell" (1892), "Spring Spate" (1897).

About 1900

Room 30:
Mikhail Aleksandrovich Vrubel (1856–1910; varied themes, sometimes with Symbolist elements): "Pan" (1899), "Seated Demon" (1890), "Fallen Demon" (1902).

Ilya Repin's "Ivan the Terrible with his Fatally Injured Son" (1882)

Rooms 31–33:
Valentin Aleksandrovich Serov (1865–1911; member of the Itinerants group from 1894; pupil of Ilya Repin; portraits, almost Expressionist in manner; mythological scenes and historical pictures): "Girl with Peaches" (1887), "Nikolay Leskov" (1894), "The Painter Konstantin Korovin" (1891).
Aleksandr Nikolaevich Benua or Benois (1870–1960; neo-Romantic; in Paris from 1926).

Room 34:
Mikhail Vasilyevich Nesterov (1862–1942; member of Itinerants group from 1896; religious scenes and realistic genre scenes; after the Revolution a member of the Socialist Realism school): "The Hermit" (1888–89), "St Bartholomew appearing to a Boy" (1890).
Also paintings by Vrubel (see Room 30).

Room 35:
Igor Emmanuilovich Grabar (1871–1960; after an Impressionist phase, painting landscapes, mainly portraits of Soviet politicians; Director of Tretyakov Gallery 1913–25; Editor and co-author of "History of Russian Art", 1909–16; author of an important biography of Repin).
Abram Efimovich Arkhipov (1882–1930; pictures of the life of tramps and peasants, with Impressionist features; portraits).

Room 37:
Nikolay Konstantinovich Roerich (1874–1947; historical pictures, stage sets, Asiatic scenes).

Socialist Realism

On 23 April 1932 the Central Committee of the Communist Party of the Soviet Union declared the transitional period in Russian art at an end and laid down Socialist Realism as the only valid guideline in literature, art and music. The first All-Union Congress of Soviet Writers in August–September 1934 adopted the following definition, which is applicable in principle also to art:
"Socialist Realism . . . demands from the artist a truthful, concrete representation of reality in its revolutionary development. The truth and historical concreteness of the artistic representation of reality must be in accord with the task of the ideological training and education of the workers in the spirit of socialism."
The criteria by which a work of art must be judged are, therefore, its realistic representation of reality and its ideological position (actually an extra-artistic principle). Thus the Critical Realism of the Itinerants can be described as Bourgeois Realism, since it is directed against bourgeois society but does not point the way out of that society into socialism. This gives us a third criterion for judging a work of art – the aspect of the (socialist) future to which it looks forward.
In the field of painting this concept offers a wide range of themes: in the first place the life of the workers and portraits of political leaders, but also scenes from the partisans' struggle, the civil war and the Second World War.

Rooms 40–52:
These rooms, devoted to Socialist Realism, have works by Abram Arkhipov, Igor Grabar (see under Room 35) and Mikhail Nesterov (Room 34), and also the following:
Aleksandr Aleksandrovich Deineka (b. 1899; graphic artist, painter and sculptor; played a major part in the decoration of Moscow's Metro stations (see entry), particularly Mayakovskaya): "The Future Pilots" (1937).
Kuzma Sergeevich Petrov-Vodkin (1878–1939; a leading Symbolist before he turned to Socialist Realism).
Martiros Sergeevich Saryan (1880–1972; Symbolist, many Oriental scenes).

Icons

For a summary of the theological basis, development of icon-painting, painting techniques and the history of icon worship see the article "Icons" in the Practical Information section.

The Tretyakov Gallery's icons are displayed in Rooms 38 and 39.
Byzantine:
"St Demetrius of Salonica" (Kiev, 12th c.).
"Deesis" from the Cathedral of the Dormition in the Kremlin (see entry).
"Virgin and Child" (Novgorod, *c.* 1200).
"Ustyug Annunciation" (Novgorod, 12th c.).
"Virgin of Vladimir" (early 12th c.): one of the most celebrated Russian icons. According to the chroniclers Andrey Bogolyubsky, brother of Yury Dolgoruky, the "founder" of Moscow, brought this wonder-working image secretly from Kiev to Vladimir in 1155. In Vladimir it was revered as the palladium of the town; then in 1395, when the Tatars were threatening Moscow, it was ceremonially transported to the capital and was credited with preserving Moscow from the Tatars. Thereafter it was revered as a national treasure. Formally, the

icon belongs to the type known as the Virgin Eleousa, in which the Child looks at his Mother, while the Virgin looks at the beholder. In the 16th c. the whole surface except the faces was painted over, but Soviet restorers were able to expose the original painting.

Novgorod:
"Elijah" (*c.* 1400).
"SS Florus and Laurus" (*c.* 1500).
"The Battle of the Men of Novgorod with the Men of Suzdal" (*c.* 1500).

Pskov/Tver:
"Elijah in the Wilderness" (13th c.).
"Exaltation of the Mother of God" (14th c.).
"Dormition of the Mother of God" (15th c.).

Feofan Grek (Theophanes the Greek, *c.* 1330–after 1405; beginning of Moscow icon-painting):
"Virgin of the Don" (end of 14th c.), painted for the Cathedral of the Dormition, Kolomna; transferred to the Cathedral of the Annunciation in the Kremlin in the 16th c. (now represented there by a copy). Like the Virgin of Vladimir, it belongs to the Eleousa type, though here the Mother looks at the Child. The icon is believed to have helped Dmitry of the Don to defeat the Tatars in the Battle of Kulikovo in 1380.
"Dormition of the Mother of God" (end of 14th c.), on the reverse of the Virgin of the Don. Christ is depicted holding the soul of his dead Mother in his hands.

Andrey Rublyov (1360/1370–1430; the greatest of the medieval Russian icon-painters):
"Trinity" (1411). This is what is known as the Old Testament Trinity, based on Genesis 18, 1–8 (Abraham entertaining the three angels unawares). The story was interpreted from an early period as a prefiguration of the Trinity. In Rublyov's icon the three angels are seated at a table, with a miniature representation of a calf (lamb?) on a dish in front of them. A tree in the background represents the oak trees of Mamre, and Abraham's tent has become an architectural structure.

Dionisy:
The icon- and fresco-painter Dionisy (Dionysius) came to Moscow at some time before 1466, and during the reign of Ivan III he painted monasteries and churches in the tradition of Rublyov. The Tretyakov has fine examples of his work: the icons (the Virgin and John the Baptist, the Archangel Michael, the Apostles Peter and Paul, St Demetrius) painted by Dionisy and his sons and assistants in 1500–02 for the Cathedral of the Nativity of the Virgin in the Ferapont Monastery, Beloozero.
There is also a fine icon of the Metropolitan Aleksey with scenes from his life in marginal panels. There is a copy of this icon in the Cathedral of the Dormition in the Kremlin (see entry), where it is described as representing the Metropolitan Pyotr.

Icons of the 16th and 17th c.:
"Triumph of the Church" (16th c.).
"Prince Shuysky" (*c.* 1630).
"Tree of the Russian Realm" (1668, Ushakov).

One of the icon rooms in the Tretyakov Gallery

SS Boris and Gleb, with scenes from their life

"Tree of the Russian Realm"

Vasnetsov House-Museum (Dom-Muzey Vasnetsova) J15

Location
13 Vasnetsov Lane
(Pereulok Vasnetsova 13)

Metro
Prospekt Mira

Opening times
Sun., Wed. and Fri. 11 a.m.–5 p.m., Thurs. 1–7 p.m., Sat. 10 a.m.–4 p.m.

The house once occupied by the painter Viktor Mikhailovich Vasnetsov (1848–1926), noted particularly for his paintings of fairy-tales, is now a museum. Vasnetsov, architect of the Tretyakov Gallery, also designed his own house: built of logs in the Old Russian or "fairy-tale" style, it has the aspect of an enchanted castle lost amid the tower blocks which have sprung up all round it.
The interior of the house and the studio have been left exactly as they were during the thirty-two years Vasnetsov lived here. On the walls are sketches, pictures of scenes from fairy-tales and legends ("Prince Ivan on the Grey Wolf", "The Frog Queen", "Kashchey the Immortal", etc.), figures of witches, designs for stage sets, etc.

Yaroslavl Station (Yaroslavsky Vokzal) L15

Location
3–5 Komsomol Square
(Komsomolskaya Ploshchad 3–5)

Metro
Komsomolskaya

The Yaroslavl Station is one of the sights of Moscow both by virtue of its striking architecture and on account of the mixture of peoples to be observed here. This is the station for Zagorsk (see Practical Information – Excursions) and Yaroslavl; but its most important function is as the starting-point of the "Transsib", the Trans-Siberian Railway which links Moscow with Vladivostok, 9300 km (5800 miles) away on the Sea of Japan.
The station, in the Old Russian style of the turn of the century, was built in 1902–04 to the design of Fyodor O. Shekhtel on the site of an earlier station of the mid 19th c. The majolica decoration on the façade was the work of the group of artists who worked on the estate of Abramtsevo, Zagorsk between the 1870s and 1890s, under the aegis of the wealthy industrialist and art patron Savva I. Mamontov, and who evolved the Russian version of Art Nouveau. Shekhtel (1859–1926) was a member of the group.

"Worker and Collective Farm Girl", in the Exhibition of Economic Achievements ▶

Practical Information

Access

By air

The easiest way to get to Moscow is to fly. There are several direct flights daily from London to Moscow's Sheremetyevo 1 International Airport (British Airways, Aeroflot), and also daily services from other European cities.
The flight from London to Moscow takes about 3¾ hours.
There are five flights each week by Aeroflot from New York to Moscow with a flight time of about 11 hours. PanAm operate four flights weekly from New York with a flight time of about 15 hours.

Group travel

The cheapest and most trouble-free method of travel is a package trip – which still leaves members of the group to go about Moscow on their own if they prefer (see Group Travel).

By rail

There are trains from major cities in Western and Central Europe to Moscow, but it is a long and tedious journey and few visitors choose this method of travel.
Many holiday packages offer three days in Moscow and three in Leningrad, travelling between the two cities by train. This appears an attractive programme but, in fact, is likely to prove tiring and frustrating, since it leaves visitors no time for looking round on their own.

By car

Few visitors choose to travel to Moscow by car, since the precise route, accommodation and intervening stopovers, if any, must be specified and paid for in advance (see Motoring and Camping).

Airport (Aeroport)

Moscow has four large airports, but visitors from the West are concerned only with Sheremetyevo 1 International Airport, some 30 km (19 miles) north-west of the city centre. The journey between the airport and the city can be done either by taxi or bus, which are available twenty-four hours a day; a taxi takes about half an hour, the bus just under an hour.

Arrival

Since everything will have been settled and paid for in advance, it might be supposed that everything should go smoothly. In practice that is not necessarily so: the following hints, therefore, may help to avoid unnecessary delays and fruitless enquiries.

Passport control

The first barrier after leaving the aircraft is the passport control. If there is the slightest uncertainty about any of the visitor's personal details this may involve a delay of anything up to an hour, to say nothing of the difficulties to which it may give rise. The passport officials work with varying degrees of meticulousness, so that some have longer queues than others. If you find that your particular queue is moving very slowly, change to another.

If your passport photograph is very old or the height shown in your passport is not accurate this may cause difficulty.

The following must be produced to the passport official: passport, visa, flight ticket, landing card. The official retains the entry visa.

Customs

After passing through passport control you must collect your luggage from the carousel and go to the customs control (see Customs Regulations), which usually goes fairly quickly. Here you must produce your passport, visa and customs declaration. When the customs official returns your passport and visa and waves you on this does not mean that you are clear: it means that he wants you to open your luggage.

Before leaving customs, make sure that you have got back your passport, visa and customs declaration.

Transfer from airport to hotel

The Intourist travel instructions simply say that you will be met at the airport. That may seem straightforward enough; but in practice there may be several hundred visitors all looking for their particular Intourist interpreter.

It is, of course, perfectly true that visitors are met at the airport. The interpreters collect small groups and take them off to their hotels; but if you have taken a long time to get through passport and customs control your interpreter may have left without you. It is no use going to one of the Intourist desks and asking about your hotel, for they will simply refer you back to the meeting-point with its milling crowd of new arrivals. The only thing to do is to keep asking any Intourist person you see: one of them will be the right one.

When looking for your interpreter you should keep in your hand the voucher which specifies the services you are entitled to and the group to which you belong. When you have found the right person, he or she will take the voucher from you.

Once the group is complete the members will be taken to their hotel by coach.

Antiques

As a general rule the export of antiques from the Soviet Union is prohibited. This general prohibition applies to antiques and works of art such as pictures, drawings, sculpture, carpets, icons, ecclesiastical objects, furniture and household aritcles, weapons, clothing, manuscripts, books, musical instruments and objects of archaeological interest.

In consequence no antiques are offered for sale in shops. The reason for these provisions lies in the principle of cultural policy to which Moscow owes its splendidly restored cathedrals, churches and monasteries, its collections of icons and its many museums: works of art should not be withheld from the public by private owners but should be available to all.

Antiques may be exported only with special permission from the Ministry of Culture and subject to a customs duty of 100 per cent of the purchase price.

Banks

Tourists do not need to depend on the ordinary banks for changing money, since all the large hotels have a branch of the State Bank which will change money at the official rate. There are also branches of the State Bank at the airports and most railway stations.

Bank for Foreign Trade

Eurocheques can be cashed only at the Bank for Foreign Trade (Vneshtorgbank), Serpukhovsky Val 8 (near the Don Monastery: Danilovskaya Metro station), on production of the necessary documents (see Currency).

Beriozka shops

The Beriozka shops, in which payment must be made in foreign currency, offer what is, compared with the general run of shops, a relatively wide range of consumer goods and foodstuffs. The souvenir departments are particularly well stocked, but there are also furs, cosmetics, jewellery, Western cigarettes and spirits, books (particularly art books), records, sets of slides and occasionally precious stones.
Make sure that you keep your receipt, for presentation at the customs is required.
Although furs are not unduly expensive in Moscow, it may be possible to find them cheaper outside the capital.
It is advisable to have plenty of small change, since shops may not be able to give change in the same currency. The major credit cards are now generally accepted in Beriozka shops.
The largest Beriozka shops are in the following hotels (for addresses, see Hotels):
Berlin, Kosmos, Leningradskaya, Metropol, National, Rossiya, Ukraina.
Many other hotels have small Beriozka shops. Before buying anything in one of these branch shops it is as well to have looked round one of the big shops first.

Bookshops (Knizhnie magaziny)

The largest bookshop in Moscow, and the one with a stock most likely to interest visitors, is:
Dom Knigi (House of the Book),
26 Kalinin Avenue (Prospekt Kalinina).
Open daily (including Sundays) 11 a.m.–8 p.m.
(Books, including art books and scientific literature, postcards, posters, slides, etc.)
Other bookshops:
Druzhba, 15 Gorky Street (Ulitsa Gorkogo): books from Eastern bloc countries
Moskva, 8 Gorky Street
Knizhnaya Lavka Pisateley, 18 Kuznetsky Most
Inostrannaya Kniga, 17 Zubovsky Boulevard and 18 Kuznetsky Most: foreign books

Cafés

Moscow has few cafés in the Western sense. What it has are snack bars of varying size with no tables to sit down at; food and drink must, therefore, be taken standing.

There are, however, some comfortable cafés where you can sit down, particularly in Kalinin Avenue (see A to Z) and Gorky Street (Ulitsa Gorkogo).

Moscow's cafés and snack bars should be avoided at the end of the working day, when they are hopelessly overcrowded and long queues form at the counters.

Ice-cream parlours

These are very different from their Western equivalents, being equipped with a doorman and a cloakroom in which customers' outdoor clothes must be deposited. They are well worth visiting for the sake of their excellent cream ices (*morozhenoe*). Some 170 tonnes (187 tons) of ice-cream are sold every day in Moscow, in winter as well as in summer – not only in cafés but outside Metro stations, at the circus, in restaurants and in department stores.

Visitors may be surprised, if they are in Moscow in winter, to see ice-cream sellers doing such a roaring trade. Once they have tasted a Moscow ice, however, they may get into the habit of eating ices in winter, too.

A Beriozka shop: the place to look for souvenirs

Calendar

Many people are surprised when they discover that the anniversary of the October Revolution is celebrated not in October but in November (see Public holidays). The explanation is that Russia switched from the Julian to the Gregorian Calendar only after the Revolution, long after the rest of Europe.

Julian Calendar (Old style)

The Julian Calendar was introduced in Russia by Peter the Great on 1 January 1700 as part of his programme for Europeanising his country. It replaced the old Byzantine era calendar (see below) to which Russia had clung long after the fall of the Byzantine Empire.
The Julian Calendar introduced by Julius Caesar from the beginning of the year 45 B.C. had eleven months of 30 or 31 days and one month (February) with 28 days and 29 in every fourth year. This gave an average length for the year of 365·25 days.

Gregorian Calendar (New Style)

In the course of the centuries the Julian year diverged significantly from the astronomical year, and in 1582, after long discussions and negotiations, Pope Gregory XIII brought the two into line in the reformed calendar which bears his name. Ten days were dropped from the Julian Calendar, so that 4 October 1582 was immediately followed by 15 October, and it was provided that the century years were not to be leap years except in years divisible by 400. The average length of the year thus became 365·2425 days, and there was no longer any significant divergence between the calendar and the astronomical year.
Italy, Spain and Portugal adopted the new calendar at once, and the other Catholic countries soon followed. The Protestant countries were more hesitant about adopting the "Papal" calendar; sometimes both methods of dating were used concurrently. By 1700, when Russia was just switching to the Julian Calendar, the Gregorian Calendar had been accepted in the German-speaking Protestant countries. It was adopted in Britain in 1752.
The Gregorian Calendar was introduced in the Soviet Union on 14 February 1918. By this time the difference between the Julian and the Gregorian Calendar had increased to 13 days: thus 25 October (Old Style), the day on which the Bolsheviks seized power, was 7 November according to the Gregorian Calendar, and this is, therefore, the day on which the anniversary of the October Revolution is celebrated.
Historians normally give dates of events in Russia before the calendar reform of 1918 according to the Julian Calendar (Old Style). Sometimes it may be convenient to give both Old Style and New Style dates.

Byzantine era calendar

The Byzantine era calendar used in Russia before 1 January 1700 took as its starting-point the date of the creation of the world, which was determined to be 1 September 5509 B.C. (according to the Gregorian calendar). Thus the supposed founding of Moscow took place, according to the chroniclers, in the year 6655 (i.e. this number of years from the creation of the world). The conversion from a Byzantine-era date to a Julian date can be exact, however, only if the month is given. For dates between January and August, 5508 years have to be subtracted from the Byzantine date to give the Julian date;

between September and December 5509 years have to be subtracted. Where the month is not known 5508 years are subtracted: thus the first mention of Moscow, dated 6655 in the Byzantine era, becomes A.D. 1147 (6655 minus 5508) in the Julian Calendar.

Camping

Camping trips in the Soviet Union can be booked either using your own tent or hiring one; hiring is only slightly dearer than taking your own tent. There are tents for two and four persons available for hire. Cabins for three or six persons are also available for hire.
Soviet camping sites have full sanitary, cooking and recreational facilities, restaurants and shops, and areas for car maintenance and washing. There are usually petrol and service stations near by.
Like all travel arrangements in the Soviet Union, camping trips must be programmed in advance, approved by Intourist (see Information) and paid for in advance. The "camping pass" which is issued when this has been done confirms the booking, and must be enclosed with the application for a visa (see Travel Documents).
The overnight charge for the use of a camping site includes the use of electricity, cooking facilities, kitchen utensils and tableware, the use of sanitary and laundry facilities and a three-hour Intourist conducted tour at each stopping-place on the route.

Moscow camping sites

Butovo
Butovo, 25 km (15 miles) south
320 beds; tel. 3 81 77 34
Open 1 June to 15 September

Mozhaisky
Mozhaiskoe Shosse 165 (16 km (10 miles) west of city centre)
206 beds; tel. 4 46 23 35
Open 1 June to 15 September

Chemists (Apteky)

The address of the nearest pharmacy can be obtained from the Intourist or information desk in any hotel.
Moscow has plenty of pharmacies, but since there are likely to be linguistic difficulties about obtaining any particular Western preparation those who require such medicines should take an adequate supply with them.

Climate

Average temperature and precipitation:

Jan −10·5 °C (13·1 °F) 47 mm (1·85 in).
Feb −9·7 °C (14·5 °F) 45 mm (1·77 in).
Mar −4·7 °C (23·5 °F) 48 mm (1·89 in). Snow begins to melt

April	4·0 °C (39·2 °F)	44 mm (1·73 in).	Ice breaks up on Moskva
May	11·7 °C (53·1 °F)	53 mm (2·09 in).	First spring storms, first apple blossom
June	16·0 °C (60·8 °F)	68 mm (2·68 in).	
July	18·3 °C (64·9 °F)	81 mm (3·19 in).	
Aug	16·3 °C (61·3 °F)	64 mm (2·52 in).	Leaves fall
Sept	10·7 °C (51·3 °F)	56 mm (2·20 in).	First night frosts
Oct	4·1 °C (39·4 °F)	56 mm (2·20 in).	First snow falls
Nov	−2·5 °C (27·5 °F)	55 mm (2·17 in).	Complete snow cover
Dec	−7·8 °C (18·0 °F)	55 mm (2·17 in).	

Concert halls

See Theatres and concert halls

Currency

Currency unit

The Soviet unit of currency is the ruble, which consists of 100 copecks.
There are banknotes for 1, 3, 5, 10, 25, 50 and 100 rubles and coins in denominations of 1, 2, 3, 5, 15, 20 and 50 copecks and 1 ruble.

Exchange rates

£1 sterling = (approx) 1·01 rubles; 1 ruble = £0·99.
$ = (approx) 0·68 rubles; 1 ruble = $1·46.
Rates may vary; they should be checked before departure.

Import of currency

The import of Russian currency is strictly prohibited.
The currency of other countries, travellers' cheques, precious metals like gold, silver and platinum and articles made from such metals (but not gold coins) may be taken into the Soviet Union without restriction.
All currency must be declared on entering the Soviet Union, and the currency declaration, duly stamped, must be carefully preserved until departure. Currency and valuables may not be taken out of the country if the currency declaration has been lost: this is the significance of the warning on the form that it will not be replaced if lost.

Changing money

Cash and other forms of currency may be changed into rubles in the branches of the State Bank in the large hotels used by foreigners. When changing money the passport, visa and currency declaration must be produced; if the passport and visa, which are handed in at reception on arrival, have not been returned the currency declaration alone may be accepted.
Money is changed at the current official rate, which is published monthly in the Press.
Make sure that you have plenty of your own currency, in small notes or even coins, since most souvenirs are bought with foreign currency (see Beriozka shops), and many restaurants also prefer Western currency to rubles. Rubles are likely to be used mainly on public transport (see entry) or for the admission charge to museums (see entry).

Soviet banknotes and coins

Export of currency

The export of Soviet currency is strictly prohibited. Foreign currency may be taken out only up to the amount declared on entry.

Unused rubles must be changed back when leaving the Soviet Union; for this purpose the receipt for the original exchange into rubles must be produced. There will of course be a loss on the double exchange.

This means in practice that the prudent visitor will change as little as possible into rubles and will try to spend all his rubles before passing through the exit controls.

Travellers cheques

Well-known travellers cheques drawn in rubles can be cashed at all exchange offices on production of passport, visa and currency declaration. Cheques drawn in foreign currency can be cashed only at the Bank for Foreign Trade (see Banks).

Credit cards

Intourist, Aeroflot, Rent-a-Car and numbers of restaurants, etc. accept the major credit cards.

Customs regulations (Tamozhnya)

Import

The following may be taken into the Soviet Union without payment of duty: personal effects, travelling requirements, sports equipment, cosmetics and a reasonable quantity of foodstuffs; two still cameras with accessories, a moving camera and accessories, a transistor radio, a portable musical instrument, a tape recorder, a portable typewriter and two watches; 250 grams of coffee, 100 grams of tea and 200 cigarettes.

Souvenirs, art books and gifts may be taken in up to a limited value in rubles.
The following may not be taken into the Soviet Union: military weapons and ammunition, gunpowder and explosives, powerful poisons, narcotics of all kinds, pornographic material and films, records or written material which are politically or economically prejudicial to the Soviet Union.
Visitors who are going to the Soviet Union to hunt (shoot) may take in a sporting gun on producing evidence of the purpose of their visit.
On arrival in the Soviet Union visitors must fill in a customs declaration. Forms are available in English and many other languages.

Export

Visitors may take out souvenirs and personal effects. In the case of valuable objects brought into the country the customs declaration must be produced on entry, in the case of furs and jewellery bought in the Soviet Union the receipt from the shop must be produced.
Antiques and *objets d'art* may be taken out only with a permit from the Ministry of Culture and on payment of a duty of 100 per cent of the value of the articles as shown in the permit.
The following may not be taken out of the Soviet Union: military weapons and ammunition, gunpowder and explosives, powerful poisons, narcotics of all kinds, old securities.

Currency

See that entry

Department stores (Univermagy)

Detsky Mir (Children's World),
2 Marx Avenue (Prospekt Marksa)
Open Mon.–Sat. 8 a.m.–9 p.m.
The largest children's store in the Soviet Union, with 16,500 sq. m (178,000 sq. ft) devoted to goods for children and young people.

GUM
See A to Z, Red Square

TsUM (Central Universal Store),
2 Petrovka Street (near Bolshoy Theatre)
Open daily 8 a.m.–9 p.m.
Moscow's largest store after GUM.

Dress

Summer

Visitors to Moscow in summer should take what they would wear in a Western European country. It should be understood, however, that the temperatures given in the entry for Climate are average figures: in the summer of 1981 peak temperatures of up to 37 °C (99 °F) were recorded.
In view of the frequent showers in summer a raincoat or umbrella should be taken.

Winter

A warm coat, warm footwear and a head-covering which should preferably go over the ears are indispensable in winter. Ankle-length fur coats are best avoided, since even in December or January there may be a sudden thaw, leaving deep puddles in the streets.
The extreme cold means that the snow is generally not very deep. The pavements and roadway are cleared several times daily, piles of snow being heaped up along the edges. In spite of regular clearance, however, chaotic snow conditions in January and February 1982 brought traffic to a complete standstill.
Long coats, therefore, should be avoided, and high boots are advisable. Boots should have non-skid soles, since under the surface covering of snow there is usually a sheet of ice. (In Moscow sand, not salt, is scattered on the streets.)

Electricity

The standard voltage in the Soviet Union is 220 volts. Sockets require a continental-type plug or adaptor.

Embassies

United Kingdom

14 Maurice Thorez Embankment (Naberezhnaya Morisa Toreza 14), tel. 2 31 85 11

United States

19–23 Tchaikovsky Street (Ulitsa Chaykovskogo 19–23), tel. 2 52 24 51–59

Canada

23 Starokonyushenny Lane (Starokonyushenny Pereulok 23), tel. 2 41 91 55

Emergency calls

Fire

Dial 01

Police

Dial 02

Medical Aid

Dial 03

Events

The programmes of all Moscow theatres and concert halls are given in a fortnightly publication (in English and other languages) available from Intourist (see Information).
The principal events, exhibitions, films (with brief summaries, useful for visitors) and sporting events are listed in the "Moscow News" (published in English, French and Spanish), which is available in newspaper kiosks for a few copecks.
A weekly brochure, "Teatralno-Kontsertnaya Moskva" (in Russia), can be obtained from theatre box-offices and usherettes. Intourist service bureaux also display theatre and concert plans covering a ten-day period (in Russian).

Excursions

For all the excursions suggested below except Kolomenskoe, which lies within the city boundaries, special permission is required, obtainable through Intourist. In the case of group excursions this is arranged by the organisers.

Abramtsevo

A mansion 60 km (37 miles) north of Moscow, near Zagorsk; once the property of the industrialist and art patron Savva I. Mamontov, who encouraged and supported a group of artists here between the 1870s and 1890s. The Abramtsevo artists' colony made a major contribution to the development of the Russian version of Art Nouveau. Church; museum.

Arkhangelskoe

A village 16 km (10 miles) west of Moscow in a beautiful setting on the river Moskva, with a late 17th c. mansion (with theatre, domestic offices and park) which is now a museum and a protected "monument of Russian 18th and 19th c. culture". The theatre has an exhibition on the Arkhangelskoe serf theatre. Restaurant, with a menu which includes bear meat and venison.

Borodino

A village 124 km (77 miles) west of Moscow, with the Borodino War Museum, commemorating the battle with the French on 26 August 1812.

Gorki Leninskie

A country house 35 km (22 miles) south of Moscow, with mementoes of Lenin.

Klin

An old Russian town (founded 1318) 84 km (52 miles) north-west of Moscow on the banks of the River Sestra. Church (16th c.), monastery in Naryshkin Baroque style. The principal attraction is the Tchaikovsky Museum.

Kolomenskoe

A huge open-air museum of architecture on the south side of Moscow, within the city limits. The best-preserved summer palace of the Tsars; Cathedral of the Ascension (1532) and several other churches; bell-tower. The whole complex is a branch of the Historical Museum (see A to Z, Red Square). Visit not recommended in bad weather (many buildings closed). There is a fine model of Kolomenskoe in the branch of the Shchusev Museum of Architecture in the Don Monastery (see A to Z).

Zagorsk

Russia's most important monastery complex, founded by St Sergius of Radonezh in 1340; in the 16th and 17th c. a great art centre (icons, book illumination, woodcarving and other crafts); since 1920 a State museum. Several churches, Metropolitan palace, Tsar's apartments, secular buildings. A visit is recommended at any time of year.

Food and drink (Eda i pityo)

Moscow is the capital not only of the Russian Soviet Federated Socialist Republic but also of a Union of fifteen Soviet Republics. Visitors can, therefore, sample, in addition to

Russian national dishes, the various specialities of Siberia, Central Asia or the Caucasus.
The Restaurant entries are listed according to their particular cuisines.
Both the midday and the evening meal consist of four courses – appetisers, soup, main dish and sweet. The meal is usually followed by either coffee or tea.
In a restaurant the whole meal, from the appetisers to the tea or coffee, is ordered at the same time.

Appetisers (*zakuski*)

Typical Russian starters are vegetable salad (Russian salad), smoked salmon, jellied sturgeon, crab salad, smoked sprats, pickled herring with onions, *bliny* (buckwheat pancakes), caviar and titbits of meat or fish in aspic. Some restaurants also serve *pirogy* (dumplings).
The appetisers may be accompanied by a glass of vodka.

Caviar

The Soviet Union is the main producer of this "black gold". Caviar, the world's most expensive foodstuff, comes from the Caspian Sea and the lower course of the Volga. It is the roe of the sturgeon, a sea fish which swims up the rivers to spawn. There are more than twenty species of sturgeon, three of which – the *beluga*, the *osyotr* and the *sevruga* – supply caviar. To maintain the annual output of just under 500 tonnes (492 tons) of caviar some 250,000 sturgeon must be caught every year; and to ensure an adequate supply of sturgeon some 70 million fry are released into breeding-ponds every year.

Species:
The female beluga weighs up to 500 kg (1100 lb) and produces 15–20 kg (33–44 lb) of large-grained caviar. Beluga is the dearest caviar and is rated the best.
The osyotr weighs an average 25–40 kg (55–88 lb) and produces 4–10 kg (9–22 lb) of caviar, slightly smaller in grain than the beluga. More of this species are caught than of beluga, and the caviar is, therefore, rather cheaper. Many people claim, however, the osyotr is better than beluga.
The sevruga weighs 9–10 kg (20–22 lb) and produces some 2 kg (4½ lb) of fine-grained caviar. It is the cheapest kind of caviar.

Eating and buying caviar:
The lighter in colour caviar is, the better. White caviar (mostly from albino sturgeon) was formerly reserved for the Tsars. Silver-grey, light brown or gold-brown caviar is rare and expensive. The commonest type is black caviar. Red caviar comes from salmon.
Caviar is never eaten with lemon. It is usually taken with buckwheat pancakes (*bliny*), potato fritters or potato pancakes. Connoisseurs eat it straight from the tin, which is set in ice, with a small mother-of-pearl, tortoiseshell or horn spoon. Caviar should always be bought in a tin, not in a glass jar. It is best only slightly salted (look for *malosol* on the label).

Soups (*supy*)

The Russians are famous for their tasty soups. A selection of the best known:
borshch: red cabbage soup, with sour cream and a dash of kvas; often regarded as the Russian national dish.
okroshka: a cold vegetable soup (dill, cucumbers, onions, garlic), with small pieces of beef and a dash of kvas.

rassolnik: beef stock with vegetables (sorrel, gherkins, celery), kidneys and sour cream.
solyanka: a sharp-flavoured vegetable soup with smoked fish (rybnaya solyanka) or meat (myasnaya solyanka).
shchi: cabbage soup.

Main course

The main course is usually in fact two courses: first fish (sturgeon, salmon, pike-perch, trout), the *pervoe blyudo* (first dish), and then meat, the *vtoroe blyudo* (second dish) – steak, minced meat in various forms, goulash (bœuf Stroganov), etc. The speciality restaurants (see Restaurants) offer a variety of other main dishes, varying from establishment to establishment.

Dessert

The favourite dessert is ice cream (*morozhenoe*), of which there are some 150 varieties. There are also many other kinds of sweet (*sladkoe*) – cakes, tarts, etc.

Wines

Recommended brands are Tsinandali (a dry white wine from Georgia), Moldavian Rose (an aromatic Moldavian red wine) and Red Star (a muscatel wine produced in the Crimea). Russian champagne is generally good.

Vodka

Vodka has long been regarded as the Russian national drink, though attempts are now being made to reduce its consumption. Like other alcoholic drinks in the Soviet Union, vodka is measured not in litres but in grams. Etiquette requires the glass to be emptied at one go. The effect can be palliated by drinking mineral water afterwards.

Kvas

Kvas, a very popular refreshing drink in summer, is made from fermented rye, buckwheat, malt, fruit and sugar. It is slightly alcoholic.
An old Russian national drink – which may appeal less to non-Russians – is kvas with horse-radish and honey.

Beer and lemonade

Russian beer is very light and an excellent thirst-quencher. Some Beriozka shops (see entry) sell Western brands of beer. Russian lemonade is best avoided.

Group travel

A package trip with a group is the cheapest way to get to Moscow. The package, in addition to the flight, accommodation and full board, may include visits to the theatre, ballet, museums, circus, etc., or a supplementary package covering these visits may be offered.
A package of this kind is well worth while for the sake of the city tour which is a regular feature of the programme, and also for visits to museums, since individual visitors may face delays or difficulties in getting in (for example to the Armoury in the Kremlin). It is not necessarily the way to see the very best of what is available in the way of entertainment, since groups do not usually have full freedom of choice and may have to accept something less than the best.
Visitors who want to get the most out of their stay in Moscow will do well, therefore, to break away from their group

whenever possible. They are free to go wherever they want in the city and make their own arrangements for entertainment. They may, of course, be lucky or they may not. Moscow's numerous theatres and concert halls offer for the most part only light entertainment, and it is not always easy to get tickets for the major attractions such as the Bolshoy. But it is worth trying; and if your hotel cannot help try applying to the Intourist head office (see Information).

Hospitals

See Medical emergencies

Hotels (Gostinitsy)

Visitors to Moscow only learn the name of their hotel after arriving at the airport. At the time of booking only the category is known, not the particular hotel. There is no question of Western-style competition between hotels.

Categories

Suite:
Three or four rooms with bath, toilet, telephone, television, radio and refrigerator. Car with driver and guide for up to six hours per day.

Luxury:
One or two rooms with bath, toilet, telephone, television, radio and refrigerator. Car with driver and guide for up to three hours per day.

First class:
Room with bath or shower, toilet and telephone. Television and radio can be hired at additional charge; most first-class rooms have a built-in radio. Three-hour city tour by Intourist bus, or similar tour with guide.

Tourist class:
Room with hot and cold water and telephone; baths, showers and toilets on the same floor.

Transfer to and from hotel

Whatever the category of room – and most hotels have rooms in more than one category – transport from and to the airport or railway station and the services of a porter are included in the price.

Registration

On arrival in the hotel visitors must hand in their passport and visa and fill in a registration form. Passports and visas are normally returned within two days.
After filling in the registration form visitors are given a chit with their room number. This should be shown to the attendant (*dezhurnaya*) in charge of the keys on each floor, who will then hand over the key. (Under present plans this system is to be done away with, and keys will be collected from reception on the ground floor.) The chit should also be shown to the porter on entering the hotel.

Hotels

The following are the principal hotels in which foreign visitors may be accommodated. Almost all of them have rooms in different categories.

Aeroflot
37 Leningrad Avenue (Leningradsky Prospekt), tel. 1 55 56 24
Metro: Aeroport

Altay
12 Gostinichnaya Ulitsa, tel. 4 82 58 79
Taxi advisable

Armenia
4 Nelinnaya Street, tel. 2 95 08 59
Metro: Ploshchad Sverdlova

Baikal
14 Selskokhozyaistvennaya Street, tel. 1 89 86 20
Nearest Metro: Botanichesky Sad

Belgrad
5 Smolensk Square (Smolenskaya Ploshchad), tel. 2 03 76 62, 2 48 66 92
Metro: Smolenskaya
921 rooms, 21 floors, lifts, air-conditioning, restaurant, bar, conference room, Intourist service desk, post office, newspaper kiosk, souvenirs

Berlin
3 Zhdanov Street (Ulitsa Zhdanova), tel. 2 25 69 10, 2 25 79 05
Metro: Kuznetsky Most, Dzerzhinskaya
90 rooms, 5 floors, lifts, restaurant, bar, Intourist service desk, post office, newspaper kiosk, souvenirs

Bucharest
1 Balchug Street, tel. 2 33 10 05, 2 33 24 36
Taxi advisable (nearest Metro Novokuznetskaya)
210 rooms, 7 floors, lifts, restaurant, Intourist service desk, post office, newspaper kiosk, souvenirs

Budapest
2/18 Petrovskie Linii Street, tel. 2 94 88 20
Metro: Ploshchad Sverdlova, Kuznetsky Most

Druzhba
53 Vernadsky Avenue (Prospekt Vernadskogo), tel. 4 32 96 29
Metro: Prospekt Vernadskogo

*Intourist
3–5 Gorky Street (Ulitsa Gorkogo), tel. 2 03 40 07–08, 2 03 01 31
Metro: Prospekt Marksa
466 rooms, 22 floors, lifts, air-conditioning, restaurant, bar, garage, swimming-pool, Intourist service desk, money-changing, post office, newspaper kiosk, souvenirs

Kievskaya
2 Kiev Street (Kievskaya Ulitsa), tel. 2 40 12 34
Metro: Kievskaya

National Hotel (left) and Intourist Hotel

*Kosmos
150 Peace Avenue (Prospekt Mira), tel. 2 86 21 23, 2 86 20 11
Metro: VDNKh
1777 rooms, 26 floors, lifts, air-conditioning, restaurant, bars, garage, swimming-pool, Intourist service desk, money-changing, post office, newspaper kiosk, souvenirs

*Leningradskaya
21–40 Kalenchovskaya Street, tel. 2 25 57 30, 2 25 55 72
Metro: Komsomolskaya
400 rooms, 28 floors, lifts, air-conditioning, restaurant, garage, Intourist service desk, money-changing, post office, newspaper kiosk, souvenirs
Built 1953; height 136 m (446 ft)

*Metropol
1 Marx Avenue (Prospekt Marksa), tel. 2 25 66 77, 2 28 07 16, 2 95 25 75
Metro: Prospekt Marksa
404 rooms, 5 floors, lifts, restaurant, bar, Intourist service desk, money-changing, post office, newspaper kiosk, souvenirs
Built 1899–1903 (architect Fyodor O. Shekhtel)

Minsk
22 Gorky Street (Ulitsa Gorkogo), tel. 2 99 14 48, 2 99 12 14
Metro: Pushkinskaya, Mayakovskaya
300 rooms, 10 floors, lifts, restaurant, garage, Intourist service desk, post office, newspaper kiosk, souvenirs

Mir
9 Bolshoy Devyatinsky Pereulok, tel. 2 52 01 40
Taxi advisable (nearest Metro Krasnopresnenskaya)

*Moskva
7 Marx Avenue (Prospekt Marksa), tel. 2 92 10 00
Metro: Prospekt Marksa
Café terrace with view of Kremlin
Built 1930 (architect Aleksey V. Shchusev)

*Mozhaiskaya
165 Mozhaiskoe Shossee, tel. 4 46 36 75
Taxi advisable
153 rooms, 11 floors, lifts, restaurants, bar, garage, sauna, conference room, Intourist service desk, post office, newspaper kiosk, souvenirs

*National
14/1 Marx Avenue (Prospekt Marksa), tel. 2 03 65 39
Metro: Prospekt Marksa
208 rooms, 5 floors, lifts, restaurant, bar, garage, Intourist service desk
Built 1903

Ostankino
29 Botantic Street (Botanicheskaya Ulitsa), tel. 2 19 54 11, 2 19 45 39
Taxi advisable (nearest Metro VDNKh)
968 rooms, 5 floors, lifts, restaurant, Intourist service desk, money-changing, post office, newspaper kiosk, souvenirs

Pekin
1–5 Bolshaya Sadovaya, tel. 2 09 24 42
Metro: Mayakovskaya
Built 1946–50

Rossiya
6 Razin Street (Utilsa Razina), tel. 2 98 54 00, 2 98 14 42
Metro: Ploshchad Nogina
1000 rooms, 23 floors, lifts, air-conditioning, restaurant, bar, garage, Intourist service desk, money-changing, post office, newspaper kiosk, souvenirs
Built 1967

Sevastopol
1A Yushunskaya Bolshaya Street, tel. 1 19 69 68
Metro: Kakhovskaya
726 rooms, 16 floors, lifts, air-conditioning, restaurant, bar, conference room, Intourist service desk, post office, newspaper kiosk, souvenirs
Also a motel; adjoining is Intourist camping site

Severnaya
50 Sushchovsky Val, tel. 2 89 12 23
Taxi advisable (nearest Metro Rizhskaya)

*Sovetskaya
32/2 Leningrad Avenue (Leningradsky Prospekt), tel. 2 50 72 53
Metro: Belorusskaya
Only for official guests and delegations

Sport
19 Lenin Avenue (Leninsky Prospekt)
700 rooms, 22 floors, lifts, air-conditioning, restaurant, bar, garage, Intourist service desk, conference room

Sputnik
38 Lenin Avenue (Leninsky Prospekt), tel. 1 25 71 06
Metro: Leninsky Prospekt

Sputnik Hotel Complex, Ismailovo
Metro: Izmailovsky Park
Five 28-storey hotels, each with restaurant, cinema and concert hall; cafés, bars, sauna, swimming-pool, telephone office, post office, underground garages, sports facilities, boat hire

Tsentralnaya
10 Gorky Street (Ulitsa Gorkogo), tel. 2 29 06 07, 2 29 08 48
Metro: Pushinskaya, Prospekt Marksa
200 rooms, 7 floors, lifts, restaurant, Intourist service desk, post office, newspaper kiosk

*Ukraina
2/1 Kutuzov Avenue (Kutuzovsky Prospekt), tel. 2 43 30 21, 2 43 27 95
Metro: Kievskaya
625 rooms, 30 floors, lifts, air-conditioning, restaurant, garage, Intourist service desk, money-changing, post office, newspaper kiosk, souvenirs
Built 1956; height 198 m (650 ft)

Ural
40 Chernyshevsky Street (Ulitsa Chernyshevskogo), tel. 2 97 42 58
Metro: Kurskaya

Varshava
2 October Square (Oktyabrskaya Ploshchad), tel. 2 33 00 32

Yaroslavskaya
8 Yaroslavl Street (Yaroslavskaya Ulitsa), tel. 2 83 17 33
Metro: VDNKh

Yunost
35 Frunzensky Val, tel. 2 42 48 61
Metro: Sportivnaya

Zarya
5 Gostinichnaya Street, tel. 4 82 23 58
Taxi advisable (nearest Metro Novoslobodskaya)

Zolotoy Kolos
15 Yaroslavl Street (Yaroslavskaya Ulitsa), tel. 2 83 16 94
Metro: VDNKh

Icons

"Thou shalt not make unto thee any graven image, or any likeness of any thing that is in heaven above, or that is in the earth beneath, or that is in the water under the earth:
"Thou shalt not bow down thyself to them, nor serve them . . ." (Exodus 20, 4–5).
The splendid arrays of icons to be seen in Moscow's churches, chapels, cathedrals and monasteries and above all in the Tretyakov Gallery (see A to Z), with its collection of icons from all over the Soviet Union, seem in flagrant contradiction of this Second Commandment: an injunction which formed the basis of the Old Testament ban on images and gave rise in Byzantine times to the Iconoclastic conflict, the results of which are basic to the understanding of Russian icons.

Portraits

The world "icon" comes from the Greek *eikon*, "image, likeness"; and the earliest icons, which probably originated in the Eastern Roman Empire, were portraits of Christ, the Virgin, saints and martyrs. A model was provided by Antique portraits of tragedians and philosophers, painted likenesses of Emperors and the portraits which bishops caused to be hung in churches.
Christianity came into being in a world (Greece, Rome, Egypt) which, with the exception of the Jews, thought well of portrait likenesses, and could not in the long run entirely reject images. But matters developed differently in the Eastern and Western Empires, a major factor no doubt being the proximity of Egypt (mummy portraits) and Syria (where the image was seen as part of the person represented). While Rome laid stress on the symbolic quality of images, with religious painting consequently able to develop unhindered in the West, in the East there was a violent conflict which led to the systematic destruction of images between 726 and 842.

Veneration of icons

In considering the Iconoclastic conflict and the present form of icons it is important to note the distinction between adoration and veneration. Only God may be adored; images may only be venerated. Veneration is expressed by *proskynesis* or bowing down before an icon, kissing it, burning incense or lighting candles; and icons may be publicly displayed or carried in procession. This veneration – which had its counterpart in the veneration of the painted image of the Emperor, the Eastern Roman Emperor being regarded from the time of Constantine the Great as Christ's representative on earth – was still more strongly felt in the case of icons regarded as wonder-working, and not infrequently took on superstitious and magical forms. According to Basil the Great, one of the great 4th c. Fathers of the Eastern Church, what was venerated was not the image itself but the person or object represented in the image. The object of veneration was not the icon but the power immanent in the sacred person or object; and conversely it was this immanent power that was transmitted to the venerator.

Iconoclasm

The controversy began in the 4th c. The supporters of images – SS Basil the Great, Gregory of Nazianzus and John Chrysostom among others – could cite in favour of their view the Epistle to the Colossians (1, 15), in which Christ is called "the image [eikon/imago] of the invisible God", seeing in this

Andrey Rublyov: "Old Testament Trinity" (left), 'Christ Pantocrator" (right)

reference a first theological justification of the image. The opponents of images – a leading role among them being taken by Eusebius of Caesarea – relied mainly on the Second Commandment.

The Emperor Leo III's Edict of 730 prohibiting the veneration of images arose – leaving aside political motives – from the fear that the venerators of images (*iconodules*) would show honour to the image but not to the reality immanent in the image. Then in 754 a Synod called by Constantine V decided that the images should be destroyed – the policy that became known as "iconoclasm". The iconodules were persecuted, tortured and executed; and almost all Byzantine icons before this period were destroyed and are lost to us.

The present Orthodox doctrine on icons was resolved at the Second Council of Nicaea (787), during the reign of the Empress Irene, on the basis of the teachings of John of Damascus ("The image is a likeness which expresses the original image in such a way that there still remains a difference"). In the words of the resolution adopted by the Council: "Representations of the Cross and sacred images, whether painted or carved and of whatever material, may appear on utensils or vestments, walls, houses or roads. Among such images are included not only those of Jesus Christ but also those of His stainless Mother, the angels and all other holy persons. It is in the nature of these images that he who contemplates them is increasingly led to recall their originals and to imitate them the more often he contemplates them; he will feel moved to show them respect and veneration but not adoration in the full sense, which belongs only to God. In token

of veneration he will offer them incense and candles, such as are due to the Holy Cross, the holy Gospel and the Church vessels. This was the pious practice of the ancients, for the honour shown to an image is shown also to him whom it represents. Therefore he who honours an image honours the person whom it represents."
Nevertheless iconoclasm flared up again in the reigns of the Emperors Leo V (813–20), Michael II (820–29) and Theophilus (829–42). Finally, however, in 842/843, the Empress Theodora reasserted the doctrine laid down by the 787 Council: an event still commemorated in the Church's calendar as the Festival of Orthodoxy.

Style

Under the doctrine laid down by the Second Council of Nicaea the icon must, ideally, represent an authentic "copy" of a historical or assumed prototype. This effort to achieve identity explains the stereotyped character of icons, for ideally an icon can be in accord with the aspect of the prototype it represents only in a single version. There are only a few basic types of Christ – the best known being the Pantocrator – but of the Mother of God there are some 200. An icon is never, however, an act of free artistic creation: if it were it would merely be an idol or graven image. The composition, the general aspect and the colours are for the most part firmly prescribed in special books.
Particularly authentic were those images which were held to be "not painted by the hand of man". The best known of these are the image of Christ associated with the legend of King Abgar of Edessa and the imprint of his face on St Veronica's "handkerchief", the Mandylion or Vernicle.
Also in this category are the likenesses of the Mother of God which were believed to have been painted from life by Luke the Evangelist. Out of these images developed the type known as the Mother of God Hodigitria (Guide), in which the Mother and Child (on the Mother's left arm) look straight at the observer, while the Mother points to the Child with her right hand. Cf. John 2, 5: "His mother saith unto the servants, Whatsoever he saith unto you, do it."
Another representation of the Virgin, with three hands, is associated with a legend about John of Damascus and the Iconoclastic controversy. It is said that the Emperor Leo III struck off one of John's hands, whereupon John prayed to the Mother of God, who restored his hand. John then presented a silver hand to the icon, and this third hand also appears in later representations.
Representations of the Virgin occupy a central position in the repertoire of the icon-painters. This followed the recognition, at the Council of Ephesus in 431, of the Virgin's status as the Panhagia Theotokos (All Holy Mother of God). The Virgin is still commonly referred to in the Orthodox Church by this title (in Russian Bogmater).

Technique

The image:
Most icons are painted in tempera on panels of non-resinous wood. The panel is covered with a layer of gesso and linen soaked in gesso in order to smooth out unevennesses in the wood, and this is followed by thin coats of chalk or alabaster boiled up with gesso. This *levkas* (from Greek *leukos*, "white") is then smoothed down to form the painting surface.
On this ground the design is sketched out, either by incision or

in red chalk or charcoal. After the gilding of those parts of the image that call for it (e.g. a saint's halo) the ground colours are applied, followed by glazes, applied in successive coats to achieve different shades and tones. The whole picture is then covered with a linseed oil varnish.
Most icons are painted in tempera: i.e. the inorganic pigments are tempered with diluted egg-yolk, honey, fig juice, beer or other binders. Icons were painted in tempera on fabric from a very early period. The icons painted in oil-colours which came into favour at the Italian Renaissance are regarded as quite inferior.
Every icon bears an inscription labelling the subject: a requirement introduced by the Second Council of Nicaea in order that icons should no longer be regarded from a purely aesthetic point of view. The use of the word in conjunction with the image referred back directly to the authentic prototype.

The frame and cover:
The depth of the successive coatings which were smoothed down to produce the painting surface gave the image a natural frame, but a separate frame was frequently also fitted. After the Iconoclastic conflict the frames were often painted with figures of saints and Prophets; later they were used for narrative scenes, for example from the life of a saint.
From the 12th c. onwards first the frames and later the background and parts of the figures began to be given metal (usually silver) covers. In the 19th c. the practice grew up in Russia of painting only those parts that were not covered by clothing (the face, the hands) and concealing all the rest under a metal cover, the clothing, etc., being depicted by embossing. The covers – which were originally votive offerings – served to protect the surface of the icons from incense, soot from candles, dust and the kisses of worshippers.

Information (Spravka, informatsiya)

Intourist

Almost the only source of information for visitors in Moscow is the State travel agency, Intourist, which, in addition to its head office, has branches in all the large hotels used by foreigners. The staff of Intourist speak English (as well as other languages).
The Intourist branches in hotels are open to all visitors, not merely to residents in the particular hotel. If the porter asks you your business the word "Intourist" will be sufficient to secure admittance.

In the United Kingdom

Intourist,
292 Regent Street,
London W1R 6QL,
tel. 01–631 1252, 580 1221

Intourist,
71 Deansgate,
Manchester M3 2BW,
tel. 061–834 0230

In the United States	Intourist, 630 Fifth Avenue, Suite 868, New York, NY 10111, tel. (212) 757 3884
In Canada	Intourist, 1801 McGill College Avenue, Suite 630, Montreal, Quebec H3A 2NA, tel. (514) 849 6394
In Moscow	Head Office: 6 Marx Avenue (Prospekt Marksa), Moscow K–9, tel. 2 03 69 62, 2 92 22 60 Open daily 9 a.m.–12 noon and 1–10 p.m. Central Excursion Bureau: Intourist Hotel, 3–5 Gorky Street (Ulitsa Gorkogo), tel. 2 03 40 08 Sputnik Travel Agency, 4 Lebyazy Pereulok
At the airport	Intourist has service desks at all airports The Aeroflot information desk is open twenty-four hours a day: tel. 1 55 50 05. Air tickets for international airlines can be obtained from the Central International Agency of Aeroflot, 49–51 Leningradskoe Shosse, tel. 1 56 80 02.

Language

Russian is the mother tongue of some 150 million people within the Soviet Union and 3·5 million outside, and the second language of another 50 million.
Visitors to Moscow will find it useful at least to know the Russian (Cyrillic) alphabet as an aid to finding their way about.

The following table gives the approximate pronunciation of the letters, which is also the method of transcription used in this Guide. The last column shows the official Soviet transcription, which is closer to the German than to the normal English system.

Alphabet		*Pronunciation*	*Soviet transcription*
А	а	a as in "father"	a
Б	б	b	b
В	в	v	v
Г	г	g as in "gag" (pronounced v in the genitive ending -ogo, -ego)	g
Д	д	d	d

Е	е	e, ye	e (after consonant) je (after vowel and at beginning of word)
Ё	ё	o, yo	o (after consonant) je (after vowel and at beginning of word)
Ж	ж	zh as in "treasure"	ž
З	з	z	z
И	и	ee (transliterated i)	i, ji
Й	й	i, y	j
К	к	k	k
Л	л	l (a "dark" l)	l
М	м	m	m
Н	н	n	n
О	о	o	o
П	п	p	p
Р	р	r	r
С	с	s	s
Т	т	t	t
У	у	oo (transliterated u)	u
Ф	ф	f	f
Х	х	kh as in "loch"	ch
Ц	ц	ts	c
Ч	ч	ch	č
Ш	ш	sh	š
Щ	щ	shch	šč
Ъ	ъ	(hard sign; not pronounced)	–
Ы	ы	y (vocalic)	y
Ь	ь	(soft sign; adds slight y sound to preceding consonant)	–
Э	э	e	e
Ю	ю	yu	u (after consonant) ju (after vowel and at beginning of word)
Я	я	ya	ja

Development of the alphabet

At some time before 862 Cyril, one of the two "Apostles of the Slavs", developed out of the Greek minuscule letters an alphabet for writing the Slavonic language, the so-called Glagolitic alphabet, in which the first Biblical texts were translated from Greek.
Some decades later a pupil of his fellow Apostle Methodius devised a simplified alphabet based on the Greek majuscule letters, which was also attributed to Cyril and named Cyrillic after him. From the 10th c. onwards this displaced the older Glagolitic, and it is still the alphabet used by the Russian Orthodox Church, marking the distinction between the Orthodox and the "Latins", the Roman Catholics and Protestants who use the Latin Alphabet.
In 1710 Peter the Great decreed that this form of Cyrillic should be replaced in secular books by a simplified Cyrillic known as the "civil alphabet" (*grazhdansky shrift*) approximating more closely to the Latin alphabet. With some further simplification in 1918, after the October Revolution, this is the alphabet still in use today.
The use of two different scripts – the older Cyrillic used by the Church and the modernised version introduced by Peter the Great – reflected the distinction between the literary language,

Church Slavonic, and the non-literary language of the people. The dichotomy was not really resolved until the 19th c., when, largely thanks to Pushkin, Russia's greatest poet, a truly national language came into being.

Libraries (Biblioteki)

Historical Library
9 Starosadsky Pereulok

Library of the Academy of Social Sciences
28/45 Krasikov Street (Ulitsa Krasikova)

Library of Foreign Literature
1 Ulyanov Street (Ulyanovskaya Ulitsa)

Library of Science and Technology
13 Kuznetsky Most

Lenin Library
See A to Z

National Archives
Kremlin Embankment (Kremlyovskaya Naberezhnaya)

Ushinsky Library
3 Tolmachovsky Bolshoy Pereulok

Lost property offices (Byuro nakhodok)

If you lose anything you should inform the person in charge of your party and the nearest Intourist information desk (see Information). If you lose documents you should also inform your embassy (see Embassies). As a rule Intourist will be prepared to make the necessary telephone calls.

Buses, trams — Tel. 2 33 00 18, ext. 139

Railway — Left luggage offices, see Railway Stations

Metro — Komsomolskaya Station, tel. 2 22 20 85

Taxis — Tel. 2 33 42 25

Markets (Rynki)

Kolkhoz markets

In the kolkhoz (collective farm) markets, which are supported by the State, kolkhozes (collective farms) and sovkhozes (Soviet farms) sell produce surplus to their planned targets and collective farm workers sell the produce of their private plots, at open market prices. These markets seem capitalist anachronisms within the Soviet system, but they undoubtedly perform a useful economic function.

Moscow's forty or so kolkhoz markets give Western visitors, too, an opportunity of seeing people from all over Russia. The stall-holders come from all parts of the country, and so profitable is the business that they no longer come in by ox-cart or horse-drawn transport but by air.

The kolkhoz

The kolkhoz is an agricultural production co-operative in which the workers hold the land and equipment in common and are given an annual output target to fulfil, of which they then share the proceeds.
Each kolkhoz worker may have a private plot of up to 1 hectare ($2\frac{1}{2}$ acres) and may keep a cow, one or two pigs, smaller livestock and two calves. The produce may be sold in the kolkhoz markets at unrestricted prices, as may any produce of the kolkhoz itself over and above targets laid down.

The sovkhoz

The sovkhoz is a large State-owned farm, which may have a work force of anything up to 600. Unlike the collective farm workers, the workers on a sovkhoz are employees; the land and equipment belong to the State. The sovkhozes, mainly engaged in cereal production and stock-farming, produce roughly half the Soviet Union's agricultural output.

Function of the kolkhoz markets

The kolkhoz markets are encouraged by the State with the object of improving the supply of foodstuffs. Although the private plots of the collective farm workers amount to under 1 per cent of the total agricultural land this "private economy" meets 35 per cent of the Soviet Union's total consumption of meat and milk, 65 per cent of potatoes, 40 per cent of vegetables and more than half the demand for eggs.

Prices

It is laid down in regulations that the prices in kolkhoz markets are not to exceed twice the price of similar products in State shops. But the corresponding products are frequently not to be found in the State shops, and accordingly the prices in the kolkhoz markets, like prices in a capitalist system, are determined by the relationship between supply and demand. The result is that the prices are horrendously high, but the people of Moscow pay them; they may grumble, but they pay. Meat bought in the kolkhoz markets costs something like four times as much as in the State shops. Against this it must be said that the kolkhoz markets offer cuts of meat never seen in the State shops. Taking the average Moscow wage as just under 200 rubles a month and setting this against prices in the kolkhoz markets, it is possible to estimate how many times in the course of a month the average Moscow worker can afford to go shopping in the kolkhoz markets: a kilogram of tomatoes or cucumbers, up to 15 rubles (in winter); a kilogram of strawberries or cherries, up to 10 rubles (spring); a kilogram of potatoes, 5 rubles or more (spring). Only in summer are the prices rather more reasonable.

Location of markets

There are either one or two markets in every district of Moscow. The following is a selection:
Bauman Market, Bauman Street (Baumanskaya Ulitsa)
Leningrad Market, 11 Chasovaya Street
Novye Cheryomushki Market, 1/42 Lomonosov Avenue (Lomonovsky Prospekt)
Central Market, Tsvetnoy Boulevard

In a kolkhoz market

Opening times

Daily 7 a.m. to 6 p.m.

Bird Market

Kalitnikovskaya Srednaya Ulitsa
Open Sat.–Sun. 8 a.m.–1 p.m.
The Moscow bird and animal market is one of the sights of the city, worth visiting for the sake of the spectacle even if you would not dream of buying any of the heterogeneous selection of animals on view – birds, fishes (plus aquaria and water plants), dogs, cats, hares, assorted small animals, etc.

Medical emergencies

Medical treatment

In case of illness apply for help to the hotel reception or Intourist service desk. Medical treatment is provided free of charge.

Duty doctor service

Dial 03.

Casualty department

Sklifosovsky Institute
Sadovaya Ring, near Kolkhoz Square (Kolkhoznaya Ploshchad)
Metro: Prospekt Mira

Medicines

There is usually a small charge for medicines dispensed. Western preparations are not available, and visitors who need particular drugs should take a supply with them.

Motoring

Documents

Visitors driving their own car must have the following: passport, with visa and records of overnight accommodation; national driving licence with insert in Russian (obtainable at first Intourist service desk after the border) or international driving licence; instructions for motorists (issued by Intourist before departure); petrol vouchers.

Insurance

Since the international insurance certificate does not apply to the Soviet Union, it is advisable to take out a short-term insurance policy covering damage to the car, third party liability and accidents with the State organisation which provides insurance cover for foreigners, Ingosstrakh, 11 Kuibyshev Street (Ulitsa Kuibysheva), Moscow.
Payment is accepted in any currency, and any claims will be met in the same currency.

Instructions for Foreign Motorists

Visitors driving their own car must follow the official "Instructions for Foreign Motorists", which require them to keep strictly to the route specified in the travel documents issued by Intourist and to observe the motor traffic regulations and the general laws and regulations of the Soviet Union.
The route specified can be altered only by arrangement with Intourist, and any change must be entered by them in the travel documents.

Traffic regulations

In general the traffic regulations of the Soviet Union are in line with those of Western European countries and the U.S. Traffic travels on the right, with overtaking on the left.

Speed limits

Within built-up areas: 60 km p.h. (37 m.p.h.)
Outside built-up areas: 90 km p.h. (56 m.p.h.)

Right of way

Traffic coming from the right has right of way, both at ordinary intersections and on roundabouts. Trams and buses have priority over other vehicles. On pedestrian crossings, marked by diagonal lines, pedestrians have absolute priority.

Seat-belts

Seat-belts must be worn. There are heavy fines for non-use.

Lights

In built-up areas with street lighting side-lights should be used, not dipped headlights.

Drink and driving

In the Soviet Union it is an offence to drive after drinking even the smallest quantity of alcohol.

Accidents, repairs

In case of accident or repairs apply to the nearest Intourist service desk.

Museums

Opening times

Opening times of the various museums are given in the entries in the A to Z section.
Since opening times vary considerably, particularly before and after public holidays and on the first and last days of the month, it is advisable to check the times with Intourist (see Information) before visiting a museum.

Historical museums

Borodino Panorama
Kutuzov Avenue (Kutuzovsky Prospekt)
Open Sat.–Thurs. 9.30 a.m.–8 p.m. (summer), 10.30 a.m.–7 p.m. (winter)
Closed Fri. and last Thurs. of month

Boyar's House (branch of Historical Museum)
10 Razin Street (Ulitsa Razina)

Frunze Central House of Air and Space Travel
4 Red Army Street (Krasnoarmeiskaya Ulitsa)
Metro: Dinamo

Historical Museum
See A to Z, Red Square

Kolomenskoe Museum
See Excursions, Kolomenskoe

Museum on the History and Reconstruction of Moscow
See A to Z

Novodevichy Convent (branch of Historical Museum)
See A to Z

St Basil's Cathedral (branch of Historical Museum)
See A to Z, Red Square

Museums on the history of the Revolution

Central Lenin Museum
See A to Z

Central Museum of the Armed Forces
2 Commune Square (Ploshchad Kommuny)

Central Museum of the Revolution
21 Gorky Street (Utilsa Gorkogo)
Open Tues. and Wed. noon–8 p.m., Fri. 11 a.m.–7 p.m., Thurs. and Sun. 10 a.m.–6 p.m.

Kalinin Museum
21 Marx Avenue (Prospekt Marksa)

Krasnaya Presnya Museum
4 Bolshevist Street (Bolshevistskaya Ulitsa)

Lenin Funeral Train Museum
1 Lenin Square (Ploshchad Lenina)
Metro: Paveletskaya

Marx-Engels Museum
5 Marx-Engels Street (Ulitsa Marksa-Engelsa)

Art museums

Don Monastery (branch of Shchusev Museum of Architecture)
See A to Z

Museum of Ceramics
Kuskovo Palace (outside the city)

Museum of Folk Art
7 Stanislavsky Street (Ulitsa Stanislavskogo)

The Gorky Museum (left) and the Tolstoy Museum (right)

Museum of Oriental Art
16 Obukh Street (Ulitsa Obukha)

Museum of Serf Art
Ostankino Palace

Pushkin Museum of Fine Art
See A to Z

Rublyov Museum of Old Russian Art
See A to Z, Andronikov Monastery

Shchusev Museum of Architecture
See A to Z

State Armoury
See A to Z, Kremlin

Tretyakov Gallery
See A to Z

Tropinin Museum
Shchetininsky Pereulok

Vasnetsov House-Museum
See A to Z

Literary museums

Chekhov House
11 Sadovaya-Kudrinskaya Street

Dostoevsky House
2 Dostoevsky Street (Ulitsa Dostoevskogo)

Gorky Memorial House
6/2 Kachalov Street (Ulitsa Kachalova)

Gorky Museum
25A Vorovsky Street (Ulitsa Vorovskogo)

Herzen Museum
Sivtsev Vrazhek Pereulok (Lane)

Literary Museum
38 Dimitrov Street (Ulitsa Dimitrova)

Mayakovsky Museum
3/6 Serov Passage (Proezd Serova)

Ostrovsky Museum
14 Gorky Street (Ulitsa Gorkogo)

Pushkin House
12/2 Kropotkin Street (Kropotkinskaya Ulitsa)

Tolstoy House
21 Lev Tolstoy Street (Ulitsa Lva Tolstogo)

Tolstoy Museum
11 Kropotkin Street (Kropotkinskaya Ulitsa)

Yermolova House
11 Tver Boulevard (Tverskoy Bulvar)

Scientific museums

Anthropological Museum
18 Marx Avenue (Prospekt Marksa)

Botanic Garden of the Academy of Sciences
4 Botanic Street (Botanicheskaya Ulitsa)

Darwin Museum
1 Pirogovskaya Malaya Street

Durov Zoo of Trained Animals
4 Durov Street (Ulitsa Durova)

Geographical Museum
Leninskie Gory (in Lomonosov University)
See A to Z, Lomonosov University

Horse-Breeding Museum
54 Timiryazev Street (Timiryazevskaya Ulitsa)

Metro Museum
See A to Z, Metro stations

Mineralogical Museum
Lenin Avenue (Leninsky Prospekt)

Museum of Palaeontology
14–16 Lenin Avenue (Leninsky Prospekt)

Museum of Physical Culture and Sport
Lenin Stadium, Luzhniki
See A to Z, Luzhniki Sports Complex

Museum of Soil Science and Agricultural Science
55 Timiryazev Street (Timiryazevskaya Ulitsa)

Museum of Space Travel
See A to Z, Exhibition of Economic Achievements

Pharmaceutical Museum
35 Krasikov Street (Ulitsa Krasikova)

Planetarium
5 Sadovaya-Kudrinskaya Street

Polytechnic Museum
See A to Z

Small Botanic Garden
26 Peace Avenue (Prospekt Mira)

Stockbreeding Museum
44 Timiryazev Street (Timiryazevskaya Ulitsa)

Timiryazev Museum of Biology
15 Gruzinskaya Malaya Street

Zoological Garden
Gruzinskaya Bolshaya Street
Metro: Barrikadnaya

Zoological Museum
6 Herzen Street (Ulitsa Gertsena)

Zhukovsky Museum
7 Radio Street (Ulitsa Radio)

Theatrical and musical museums

Bakhrushin Theatrical Museum
31/12 Bakhrushin Street (Ulitsa Bakhrushina)

Glinka Museum of Musical Culture
5 Fadeev Street (Ulitsa Fadeeva)

Gorky Arts Theatre Museum
3 Arts Theatre Passage (Proezd Khudozhestvennogo Teatra)

Nemirovich-Danchenko Museum
5 Nemirovich-Danchenko Street (Ulitsa Nemirovicha-Danchenko)

Skryabin Museum
11 Vakhtangov Street (Ulitsa Vakhtangova)

Stanislavsky House-Museum
6 Stanislavsky Street (Ulitsa Stanislavskogo)

Night life

Night life as it is known in the cities of the West does not exist in Moscow. Moscow people look for their evening's entertainment to the large restaurants (see entry) with their elegant and relaxed atmosphere, their floor shows and their orchestras for dancing.

The principal restaurants with floor shows are the following:

Arbat
21 Kalinin Avenue (Prospekt Kalinina)
Taxi advisable
Seating for 2000; from 8 p.m. variety and folk shows and dancing; in the basement "hot rhythms" for the young and the young at heart, advisable to book (through Intourist).

"Starry Sky" (Zvyozdnoe Nebo)
Ground Floor of Intourist Hotel
3–5 Gorky Street (Ulitsa Gorkogo)
Metro: Prospekt Marksa
From about 8 p.m. floor show (artistes, singers, conjurers, etc.)

Hard currency bars

Moscow has a number of bars catering exclusively to foreign visitors in which payment must be made in hard currency. Cheques and credit cards are also accepted. The word "bar" is to be taken literally: nothing is served but drinks.
The principal hard currency bars are those in the Berlin, Intourist, Metropol and National Hotels (for addresses, see Hotels).
Hard currency bars stay open at least until midnight; a few are open until morning.

Photography

Permitted

With the exceptions mentioned below, amateur photographers may photograph or film anything they wish in the Soviet Union. If they want to take photographs or make films for commercial use they should consult Intourist.
In industrial, agricultural and administrative establishments the permission of the manager or director should be obtained, and before photographing individuals their agreement should be sought.

Prohibited

The photographing or filming of military and industrial installations, airports, railway stations, bridges and radio stations is prohibited, and there is an absolute ban on photography or filming in border areas. Photography is not permitted in shops or in most cathedrals and churches.

Film

Photographers should take an adequate supply of film with them, since Western 35 mm and Super 8 film can be bought only in some Beriozka shops (see entry) and Polaroid film is not available at all.

Photographic shops

Still cameras, moving cameras and accessories, as well as sets of colour slides of Moscow and other Soviet cities, can be bought in Beriozka shops (see entry) and in the following branches of the Jupiter chain of shops:
25 Gorky Street (Ulitsa Gorkogo)
Kalinin Avenue (Prospekt Kalinina)
44 Komsomol Avenue (Komsomolsky Prospekt)
3 Lenin Avenue (Leninsky Prospekt)
15 Petrovka

Moscow's largest bookshop, the Dom Knigi (see Bookshops), has a section devoted to colour slides.

Postal services (Pochta)

Stamps

Stamps can be bought at the postal desks of hotels and at all newspaper kiosks as well as in post offices.

Postage rates

To any European country:
letters up to 20 grams (by air) 45 copecks
postcards (by air) 35 copecks

Post offices

Head Post Office
26A Kirov Street (Ulitsa Kirova)
tel. 2 28 63 11, 2 26 26 57
Open daily 8 a.m.–10 p.m.

Post-box (for inland mail)

Telecommunications House

Telecommunications House
22 Kalinin Avenue (Prospekt Kalinina)
tel. 2 02 03 01
Open daily 8 a.m.–8 p.m.

International post offices:
10 Komsomol Square (Komsomolskaya Ploshchad)
37 Varshavskoe Shosse
Open daily 9 a.m.–8 p.m.

There are some 700 smaller post offices in Moscow, and in addition almost all the hotels used by foreigners have a postal desk (sub post office).

Poste restante

Mail should be addressed c/o Intourist, Moscow K600. This is the address of the post office in the Intourist Hotel, 3 Gorky Street, where mail can be collected. The post office is open Mon.–Fri. 9 a.m.–noon and 1–8 p.m., Sat. and Sun. 9 a.m.–noon and 1–6 p.m.

Telephoning, telegrams

See respective entries

Public holidays (Prazdniki)

1 January (New Year's Day)
8 March (International Women's Day)
1–2 May (International Labour Day)
9 May (Victory in Europe Day)
7 October (Constitution Day)
7–8 November (Anniversary of October Revolution)
On public holidays museums and shops (except food shops) are closed.

Public transport (Sredstva soobshcheniya)

Metro

The quickest and most convenient form of public transport in Moscow is the Underground (Metro), with 115 stations in all parts of the city and the outer districts. The present network of some 200 km (125 miles) is constantly being extended, and is planned to reach a total length of almost 400 km (250 miles) by the year 2000.
The stations are indicated by a red "M", which is illuminated at night.
Even if you do not intend to travel on the Metro it is worth while visiting one or two of the stations (see A to Z, Metro Stations).

Travelling on the Metro

Travellers on the Metro must find their own way about. It is essential, therefore, to be able to decipher the Cyrillic alphabet (though some of the stations most used by visitors have plans giving the names of stations in the Latin alphabet).
A general idea of the system can be gained from the plan of the Metro on p. 176 of this Guide. The colours on the plan are the actual colours of the various lines: thus if you want to go from the Belorusskaya Station to Mayakovskaya you

Military parade in Red Square

Parade of sportswomen on the anniversary of the October Revolution

must take the green line. Half-way along every platform is a board in the colour of the particular line showing the stations in the direction of travel.

Operating times

The Metro runs from 6 a.m. to 1 a.m. the next morning (6 a.m. to 2 a.m. on public holidays).
The Metro carries almost 6 million passengers every day. The rush hours are between 7 and 9 in the morning and 4 and 6 in the evening. At rush hours there are trains every 90 seconds; at normal times the interval is about 2 minutes on all lines. At the end of every platform are two illuminated clocks, one showing the time in hours, minutes and seconds, the other indicating the time that has elapsed since the last train.

Paying the fare

A journey on the Metro costs 5 copecks, whatever the distance and whatever the number of changes. You must pay again only if you pass the exit barrier and thus break the journey. Thus a sightseeing trip round Metro stations costs only 5 copecks, there and back.
There are no tickets: a 5-copeck coin is all you need. At the entrance to all Metro stations are change machines which change larger coins into 5-copeck pieces, and money can also be changed at the cash desk. To save time, however, it is advisable always to have plenty of small change.
The 5-copeck piece is put into the slot at the entrance barrier. If the wrong coin is inserted or if you try to go through without paying the barrier will lock.

Transferring

Those using the Metro for the first time may find changing from one line to another something of a problem; and even when you have grasped the principle changing can still be a time-consuming process.
As an example, suppose that you have travelled on the red line to the Marx Avenue (Prospekt Marksa) Station and want to go on to Smolenskaya on the dark blue line. There is no connection from the Prospekt Marksa Station, and it is, therefore, necessary to walk along the underground passage to the Ploshchad Sverdlova (Sverdlov Square) Station, and then from there to Ploshchad Revolutsii (Revolution Square), which is on the dark blue line. If you look at the city plan and see how far apart these three stations are you will get some idea of the distances you may have to walk when changing stations on the Metro.

Buses and trams

Moscow's other forms of public transport, apart from taxis (see entry), are buses, trolleybuses and (in the outer districts) trams. On account of the possible linguistic difficulties involved and the chronic overcrowding, the use of buses and trams is not recommended for foreign visitors.

Buses

Buses operate from 6 a.m. to 1 a.m. on the following morning.
Fare: 5 copecks within Moscow; in outer districts according to distance.

Trolleybuses

Trolleybuses run from 5 a.m. to 2 a.m. the next morning.
Fare: 4 copecks, irrespective of distance.

Trams

Trams are in service from 5.30 a.m. to 1 a.m. on the following morning.
Fare: 3 copecks, irrespective of distance.

Buses and trams are almost exclusively driver-only, without conductors. The fare is put into a machine beside the driver or at the rear entrance and a ticket is issued automatically. There are no change machines.

Railway stations (Vokzaly)

Moscow has nine main-line termini, with nine electrified lines from all parts of the Soviet Union. Although foreigners cannot leave the city without special permission (arrangements made through Intourist: see Information), the stations are worth visiting for the sake of the medley of nationalities to be seen there (e.g. at the Yaroslavl Station, the terminus of the Trans-Siberian).

All the stations lie between the Garden (Sadovaya) ring and the motorway ring, most of them close to the Garden ring. They are thus easily reached by Metro.

Some of the stations date from the 19th c., but most of them are in the Old Russian style of the turn of the century.

Belorussian Station (Belorussky Vokzal)
Ploshchad Belorusskogo Vokzala
Metro: Belorusskaya
Trains to Minsk and Western Europe
Built 1909, in Old Russian style

Kazan Station (Kazansky Vokzal)
2 Komsomol Square (Komsomolskaya Ploshchad)
Metro: Komsomolskaya
Trains to Kazan, the Urals and Central Asia

Kiev Station (Kievsky Vokzal)
Ploshchad Kievskogo Vokzala
Metro: Kievskaya
Trains to Prague, Bucharest, Belgrade, Budapest and Kiev
Built 1914–17

Kursk Station (Kursky Vokzal)
Ploshchad Kurskogo Vokzala
Metro: Kurskaya
Trains to Ryazan, the Crimea, the Caucasus and Kharkov

Leningrad Station (Leningradsky Vokzal)
Komsomol Square (Komsomolskaya Ploshchad)
Metro: Komsomolskaya
Trains to Leningrad, Murmansk and Finland
Moscow's oldest station, built in 1851 for the new Moscow–St Petersburg line (architect Konstantin A. Thon)

Paveletsk Station (Paveletsky Vokzal)
Lenin Square (Leninskaya Ploshchad)
Metro: Paveletskaya
Trains to Kursk, Kharkov, Simferopol, Erevan and Baku
Built 1900
Adjoining the station is the Lenin Funeral Train Museum (see Museums)

Riga Station (Rizhsky Vokzal)
Ploshchad Rizhskogo Vokzala
Metro: Rizhskaya
Trains to Riga and Volokolamsk
Built 1899, in Old Russian style

Savyolovo Station (Savyolovsky Vokzal)
Ploshchad Butyrskoy Zastavy
Nearest Metro: Novoslobodskaya
Trains to Dmitrov and Dubna
Built about 1900

Yaroslavl Station (Yaroslavsky Vokzal)
see A to Z

Restaurants (Restorany)

Many of Moscow's restaurants are in hotels. In these, and in the speciality restaurants, it is advisable to book a table in advance. Intourist will usually arrange this, even when the restaurant says it is fully booked, if payment is made in hard currency. In the restaurant of your own hotel booking is not necessary, since every guest has his place reserved at a specified time.

Opening times

Grills and restaurants are usually open from noon to 3 p.m. and from 7 to 11 p.m.

Belorussian Station

International cuisine

Belgrad I, 5 Smolensk Square (Smolenskaya Ploshchad), tel. 2 48 67 13
Belgrad II, 8 Smolensk Square, tel. 2 48 26 96
Berlin, 3 Zhdartsov Street (Ulitsa Zhdartsova), tel. 2 23 35 81
Bucharest, 1 Balchug Street, tel. 2 23 78 54
Budapest, 2/18 Petrovskie Linii, tel. 2 21 40 44
Havanna, 88 Lenin Avenue (Leninsky Prospekt), tel. 1 38 00 91
Pekin, 1/7 Sadovaya Bolshaya Street, tel. 2 09 18 65
Praga, 2 Arbat, tel. 2 90 61 71
Sedmoe Nebo (Seventh Heaven), Ostankino Television Tower
Sofia, 32 Gorky Street (Ulitsa Gorkogo), tel. 2 51 49 50
Varshava, 2/1 October Square (Oktyabrskaya Ploshchad), tel. 2 37 21 10

Russian specialities

Arbat, 29 Kalinin Avenue (Prospekt Kalinina), tel. 2 91 14 03
Bega, 22 Begovaya Street, tel. 2 56 15 66
Druzhba, 53 Vernadsky Avenue (Prospekt Vernadskogo), tel. 4 32 99 39
Intourist, 3–5 Gorky Street (Ulitsa Gorkogo), tel. 2 03 95 97
Kosmos, 150 Peace Avenue (Prospekt Mira), tel. 2 83 85 16
Leningrad, 21/40 Kalanchovskaya Street, tel. 2 08 20 27
Metropol, 1 Marx Avenue (Prospekt Marksa), tel. 2 28 40 60
Minsk, 22 Gorky Street (Ulitsa Gorkogo), tel. 2 29 12 48
Moskva, 7 Marx Avenue (Prospekt Marksa), tel. 2 92 62 67
National, 1 Gorky Street (Ulitsa Gorkogo), tel. 2 03 55 95
Okean, in the Exhibition of Economic Achievements (VDNKh), Peace Avenue (Prospekt Mira), tel. 1 81 91 45
Olimpiada, Lenin Stadium, tel. 2 45 87 23
Ostankino, 26 Botanicheskaya Street, tel. 2 19 28 09
Rossiya, 6 Razin Street (Ulitsa Razina), tel. 2 98 05 32
Slavyansky Bazar, 17 25th October Street (Ulitsa 25-ogo Oktyabrya), tel. 2 21 18 72
Stolichny, 7 Marx Avenue (Prospekt Marksa), tel. 2 92 38 08
Zolotoy Kolos, in the Exhibition of Economic Achievements (VDNKh), Peace Avenue (Prospekt Mira), tel. 1 81 94 09

Georgian specialities

Alma Ata, 13 Shvernik Street (Ulitsa Shvernika), tel. 1 27 32 83
Aragvi, 6 Gorky Street (Ulitsa Gorkogo), tel. 2 29 37 62
Ararat, 4 Neglinnaya Street, tel. 2 95 92 12
Baku, 24 Gorky Street (Ulitsa Gorkogo), tel. 2 99 85 06
Razdan, 18 Stoleshnikov Pereulok, tel. 2 21 51 50

Ukrainian and Uzbek specialities

Tashkent, in the Exhibition of Economic Achievements (VDNKh), Peace Avenue (Prospekt Mira)
Ukraina, 2/1 Kutuzov Zvenue (Kutuzovsky Prospekt), tel. 2 43 30 11
Uzbekistan, 29 Neglinnaya Street, tel. 2 94 60 53

Shopping

In all shops and department stores customers have first to go to the sales counter and choose what they want to buy, then go to the cash desk and pay the price, and finally return to the counter with the receipt and collect their purchase. For foreigners not speaking Russian the best way is to get the sales person to write down the price and show this to the clerk at the cash desk.

If the cash desk serves a number of different counters you must point out the counter where you have made your purchase.

Opening times

Shops are open daily, except on Sundays and public holidays, from 9 or 10 in the morning to 8 or 9 at night.
Most food shops are also open on Sunday.
Almost all shops are closed on either the first or the last day of the month.

The large department stores are open from 8 a.m. to 9 p.m., Monday to Saturday.

Beriozka shops, department stores, souvenirs

See respective entries

Amber

Yantar, 13 Stoleshnikov Pereulok

Arts and crafts

46 Gorky Street (Ulitsa Gorkogo)
9 Kutuzov Avenue (Kutuzovsky Prospekt)
12 Petrovka
6 Ukrainsky Bulvar

Books

See Bookshops

China

Dom Farfora, 36 Lenin Avenue (Leninsky Prospekt)

Crystal and glass

15 Gorky Street (Ulitsa Gorkogo)
8/2 Kirov Street (Ulitsa Kirova)

Food shops

Moscow's largest food shops are:
No. 1, 14 Gorky Street (Ulitsa Gorkogo)
No. 2, 54/2 Arbat
No. 3, 7 Marx Avenue (Prospekt Marksa)
No. 15, 1 Ploshchad Vosstaniya
No. 24, 64 Gorky Street (Ulitsa Gorkogo)
No. 70 (Sputnik), 32 Lenin Avenue (Leninsky Prospekt)
Novoarbatsky, 21 Kalinin Avenue (Prospekt Kalinina)

Furs

13–15 Stoleshnikov Pereulok

Gifts

Gifts can be found in the large department stores and the Beriozka shops (see entry). The Podarki chain of shops specialises in gifts. The following are among their branches:
4 Gorky Street (Ulitsa Gorkogo)
29 Kalinin Avenue (Prospekt Kalinina)
10 Michurin Avenue (Michurinsky Prospekt)
13–15 Stoleshnikov Pereulok

Also:
Tysyacha Melochey (A Thousand Trifles), 39/1 Lenin Avenue (Leninsky Prospekt)

Jewellery

Malakhitova Shkatulka, 24 Kalinin Avenue (Prospekt Kalinina)
12 Gorky Street (Ulitsa Gorkogo)
There is usually also a large selection of jewellery in the Beriozka shops (see entry).
The receipt must be kept, since it must be produced at the customs control when leaving the country.

Linen

Russky Lyon, 29 Komsomol Avenue (Komsomolsky Prospekt)

Musical instruments, etc.

Musical instruments are a good buy. There is a musical instruments department in the Detsky Mir store (see Department stores). The following shops can also be recommended:

13 Herzen Street (Ulitsa Gertsena)
15 Gorky Street (Ulitsa Gorkogo)
8/1 Neglinnaya Street

Perfume

6 Gorky Street (Ulitsa Gorkogo)
Siren, 44 Kalinin Avenue (Prospekt Kalinina)

Photographic material

See Photography

Records

Melodiya, 40 Kalinin Avenue (Prospekt Kalinina)

Shoes

Dom Obuvi, 34/1 Lenin Avenue (Leninsky Prospekt)

Souvenirs

See entry

Sports and camping equipment

No. 15, 44 Komsomol Avenue (Komsomolsky Prospekt)

Stamps

Filateliya No. 1, 1/1 Taras Shevchenko Embankment (Naberezhnaya Tarasa Shevchenko)
Filateliya No. 20, 23 Volgin Street (Ulitsa Volgina)

Also:

32/22 Chekhov Street (Ulitsa Chekhova)
92 Lenin Avenue (Leninsky Prospekt)
59 Vernadsky Avenue (Prospekt Vernadskogo)

Tea and coffee

9 Kirov Street (Ulitsa Kirova)

Textiles

Dom Tkani, 41 Lenin Avenue (Leninsky Prospekt)

Toys

Detsky Mir, see Department stores
Dom Igrushky, 8 Kutuzov Avenue (Kutuzovsky Prospekt)

Souvenirs (Suveniry)

Typical souvenirs from the Soviet Union are ceramics, woodcarving and articles carved from bone, painted wooden articles, intricately worked metal objects, filigree work, enamels, embroidery and carpets. Soviet craft products have won high distinctions at international exhibitions.

Popular, too, are the plump "matryoshka" dolls, with five, six or more smaller dolls inside. Unusual souvenirs are the miniature paintings from Palekh, the brooches, trays and caskets from Fedoskino with vividly coloured decoration on fairy-tale themes, and the bowls, jugs and spoons made in Khokhloma, painted predominantly in red and gold.

The best places for souvenirs are the gift shops of the Podarki chain (see Shopping, Gifts) and the large Beriozka shops, as well as the Russky Suvenir shop at 9 Kutuzov Avenue (Kutuzovsky Prospekt).

If you buy souvenirs of any value it is advisable to keep the receipt.

Taxis (Taxi)

Taxis are the most important form of public transport in Moscow after the Metro (see Public transport). They are available day and night.
Moscow's taxis are usually yellow, with a narrow chequered band round the sides or on the roof. A green light behind the windshield indicates that they are free.
Taxi stands are marked with a board bearing the letter "T". Taxis may also be hailed in the street, though they may sometimes be reluctant to stop.

Fares

In spite of the rise in oil prices, fares are still quite reasonable. The hire charge is 20 copecks, plus 20 copecks per kilometre. There is no extra charge for luggage. Waiting time is charged at 2 rubles per hour. All taxis have meters.

Taxi-buses

There are also taxi-buses, which run on fixed routes from 9 a.m. to 9 p.m. The fare is 15 copecks irrespective of distance.

Booking a taxi

Taxis can be ordered in advance from the following numbers:
2 25 00 00
2 27 00 40
4 57 90 05
1 37 00 40
1 57 00 40
1 67 90 11
To call a taxi from your hotel, ask Intourist. The term "in advance" should be taken literally: at least an hour should be allowed before the taxi arrives.

Private enterprise taxis

Drivers and owners of private cars sometimes like to earn a little extra money by running an unofficial taxi service. It is perfectly safe to accept the offer of a lift in this way, but the fare should be agreed in advance.

Telegrams (Telegrammy)

Telegraph Office

Central Telegraph Office
7 Gorky Street (Ulitsa Gorkogo)
tel. 2 94 47 58
Open twenty-four hours

Telephoning a telegram

Dial 2 25 20 02

Rates

Telegram: 60 copecks per word
Letter-telegram: 30 copecks per word
(Increases likely)

Telephoning (Telefonirovat)

Local calls

Local calls from the telephone in your hotel room are free. For a call from a coin-operated telephone you need a 2 copeck piece or two single copecks.

International calls

Dial 07. The call can be booked in English or French as well as Russian. In order to avoid a long wait you should give the time at which you would like the call to come through.

Information

The telephone information service can be called by dialling 09; but the operators speak only Russian. Information in foreign languages can be obtained by dialling 2 71 91 03. Another possibility is to apply to one of the information bureaux (see Information). Telephone directories are practically impossible to find.

Telephone offices

Telecommunications House,
22 Kalinin Avenue (Prospekt Kalinina),
tel. 2 02 03 01
Open daily 8 a.m.–8 p.m.

Telephone Office,
19 Gorky Street (Ulitsa Gorkogo)
Open daily 8 a.m.–11.30 p.m.

Theatres and concert halls (Teatry, kontsertnye zaly)

Arts Theatre (Old House), 3 Arts Theatre Passage (Proezd Khudozhestvennogo Teatra)
Arts Theatre (New House), 24 Tver Boulevard (Tverskoy Bulvar)
Bolshoy Theatre, Sverdlov Square (Ploshchad Sverdlova)
Central Concert Hall, Rossiya Hotel, 1 Moskva Embankment (Moskvoretskaya Naberezhnaya)
Children's Musical Theatre, 17 25th October Street (Ulitsa 25-ogo Oktyabrya)
Circus (Old Building), 13 Tsvetnoy Boulevard
Circus (New Building), 7 Vernadsky Avenue (Prospekt Vernadskogo)
Gogol Theatre, 8 Kazakov Street (Ulitsa Kazakova)
Maly (Little) Theatre, 1 Sverdlov Square (Ploshchad Sverdlova)
Mayakovsky Theatre, 19 Herzen Street (Ulitsa Gertsena)
Miniature Theatre, 3 Karetny Ryad
Mossovet Theatre, 16 Sadovaya Bolshaya Street
Oktyabr (October) Cinema and Concert Hall, 42 Kalinin Avenue (Prospekt Kalinina)
Operetta Theatre, 6 Pushkin Street (Pushkinskaya Ulitsa)
Palace of Congresses, see A to Z, Kremlin
Puppet Theatre, 26 Spartakovskaya Street
Pushkin Theatre, 23 Tver Boulevard (Tverskoy Bulvar)
Satirical Theatre, 18 Sadovaya Bolshaya Street
Stanislavsky Theatre, 23 Gorky Street (Ulitsa Gorkogo)
Taganka Theatre, 76 Chkalov Street (Ulitsa Chkalova)
Tchaikovsky Concert Hall, 31 Gorky Street (Ulitsa Gorkogo)
Television Theatre, 1 Zhuravlyov Square (Ploshchad Zhuravlyova)
Vakhtangov Theatre, 26 Arbat
Variety Theatre, 20/2 Bersenev Embankment (Bersenevskaya Naberezhnaya)
Varshava Cinema and Concert Hall, 10 Leningradskoe Shosse

Ticket agencies

Moscow has no ticket agencies in the Western sense. Their function is performed by Intourist (see Information).

Time

Moscow time is 3 hours ahead of Greenwich Mean Time and 8 hours ahead of New York time. In summer the clock is put forward an hour.

Tipping

Since the Revolution there has officially been no tipping in the Soviet Union. Service charges are included in all prices, and there is no charge for the (obligatory) use of cloakroom facilities in museums, theatres, restaurants, etc.
With increasing numbers of foreign visitors, however, waiters, taxi-drivers and porters have come to expect some small additional recognition of their services. This should generally not exceed 5–10 per cent.
Intourist staff are not allowed to accept money. The best way to express appreciation of the services of your guide, interpreter or driver is to offer him or her a small gift. Such gifts should preferably be from the West, and it is a good idea, therefore, to take some suitable items (nylons, tights, ball-point pens, cigarette lighters, etc.) from home with you. Suitable gifts can also be found in the Beriozka shops (see entry).
Over-generous gifts may appear like an attempt at bribery. The best plan, therefore, is to make any such gifts after some days or at the end of the trip.

Travel documents

All visitors to the Soviet Union must have a valid up-to-date passport and a Soviet tourist visa. British citizens must have a full 10-year passport: a British Visitor's passport is not sufficient. All passports must be valid for three months beyond the date of return from the Soviet Union.
Application must be made for a visa on the official application form, which can be obtained from Intourist or through a travel agent. The visa itself is free, but Intourist makes a small service charge. The application must be accompanied by three identical passport-type photographs and clear photostat copies, trimmed to size, of the first five pages of the applicant's passport.
The application must be sent to Intourist not earlier, or later, than 10 weeks before departure (three weeks in the case of late bookings).
The visa is a separate document, and there are no stamps or entries in the passport itself.

Car papers

See Access (by car).

Useful Telephone Numbers

Emergencies	
Fire	01
Police	02
Medical emergency service	03
Information	
Intourist	2 03 69 62, 2 92 22 60
Flight information	1 55 50 50
Rail information	2 66 99 00
Embassies	
United Kingdom	2 31 85 11
United States	2 52 24 51–59
Canada	2 41 91 55
Telephone	
Information, Moscow	09
International calls	07
Programmes of theatres and cinemas	05
Telegrams	
Telephoning a telegram	2 25 20 02

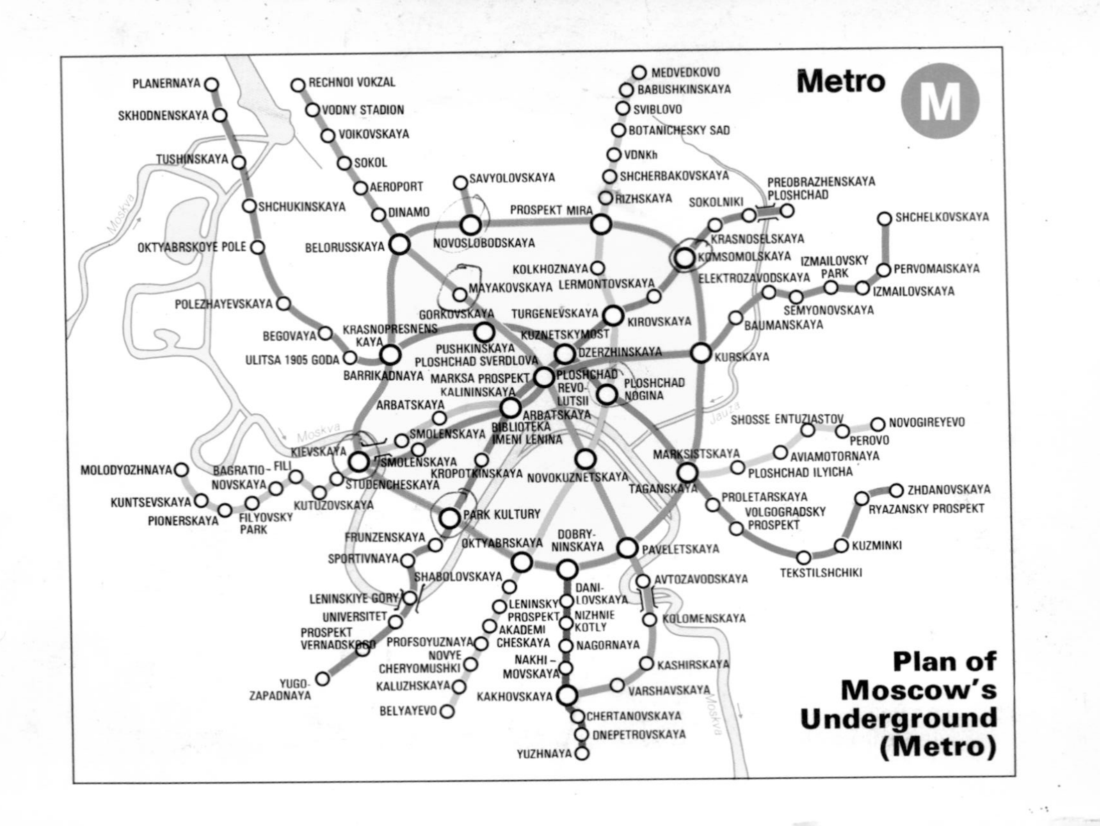
Metro
M
Plan of Moscow's Underground (Metro)
PLANERNAYA
SKHODNENSKAYA
TUSHINSKAYA
SHCHUKINSKAYA
OKTYABRSKOYE POLE
POLEZHAYEVSKAYA
BEGOVAYA
ULITSA 1905 GODA
RECHNOI VOKZAL
VODNY STADION
VOIKOVSKAYA
SOKOL
AEROPORT
DINAMO
BELORUSSKAYA
SAVYOLOVSKAYA
NOVOSLOBODSKAYA
PROSPEKT MIRA
MEDVEDKOVO
BABUSHKINSKAYA
SVIBLOVO
BOTANICHESKY SAD
VDNKh
SHCHERBAKOVSKAYA
RIZHSKAYA
PREOBRAZHENSKAYA PLOSHCHAD
SOKOLNIKI
KRASNOSELSKAYA
KOMSOMOLSKAYA
SHCHELKOVSKAYA
PERVOMAISKAYA
IZMAILOVSKY PARK
IZMAILOVSKAYA
ELEKTROZAVODSKAYA
SEMYONOVSKAYA
BAUMANSKAYA
KURSKAYA
KOLKHOZNAYA
LERMONTOVSKAYA
MAYAKOVSKAYA
GORKOVSKAYA
TURGENEVSKAYA
KIROVSKAYA
KRASNOPRESNENS KAYA
PUSHKINSKAYA
KUZNETSKY MOST
DZERZHINSKAYA
PLOSHCHAD SVERDLOVA
BARRIKADNAYA
MARKSA PROSPEKT
PLOSHCHAD REVO-LUTSII
PLOSHCHAD NOGINA
KALININSKAYA
ARBATSKAYA
ARBATSKAYA
BIBLIOTEKA IMENI LENINA
SMOLENSKAYA
SMOLENSKAYA
KIEVSKAYA
KROPOTKINSKAYA
NOVOKUZNETSKAYA
MARKSISTSKAYA
TAGANSKAYA
SHOSSE ENTUZIASTOV
PEROVO
NOVOGIREYEVO
AVIAMOTORNAYA
PLOSHCHAD ILYICHA
ZHDANOVSKAYA
RYAZANSKY PROSPEKT
KUZMINKI
TEKSTILSHCHIKI
VOLGOGRADSKY PROSPEKT
PROLETARSKAYA
MOLODYOZHNAYA
KUNTSEVSKAYA
PIONERSKAYA
BAGRATIO-NOVSKAYA
FILI
FILYOVSKY PARK
KUTUZOVSKAYA
STUDENCHESKAYA
PARK KULTURY
FRUNZENSKAYA
SPORTIVNAYA
OKTYABRSKAYA
DOBRY-NINSKAYA
PAVELETSKAYA
AVTOZAVODSKAYA
KOLOMENSKAYA
KASHIRSKAYA
VARSHAVSKAYA
SHABOLOVSKAYA
LENINSKIYE GORY
UNIVERSITET
PROSPEKT VERNADSKOGO
YUGO-ZAPADNAYA
LENINSKY PROSPEKT
AKADEMI CHESKAYA
PROFSOYUZNAYA
NOVYE CHERYOMUSHKI
KALUZHSKAYA
BELYAYEVO
DANI-LOVSKAYA
NIZHNIE KOTLY
NAGORNAYA
NAKHI-MOVSKAYA
KAKHOVSKAYA
CHERTANOVSKAYA
DNEPETROVSKAYA
YUZHNAYA
Moskva
Moskva
Moskva
Jauza